Bridge Humor

Edwin B. Kantar

Published by
Melvin Powers
WILSHIRE BOOK COMPANY
12015 Sherman Road
No. Hollywood, California 91605
Telephone: (213) 875-1711

Printed by

HAL LEIGHTON PRINTING COMPANY
P.O. Box 3952
North Hollywood, California 91605
Telephone: (213) 983-1105

Printed in the United States of America
Library of Congress Catalog Card No: 77-77690
ISBN 0-87980-342-8

Contents

Foreword

My good friend Claire Berman has been telling me for years that I should be collecting all my humorous articles (one, two?) and put them in book form.

So I did it. I went back over all my Bridge World, Popular Bridge and Sports Illustrated articles desperately searching for those that had a few chuckles.

What you are holding is what I have come up with. With the exception of three articles: "The First Board," which is to be taken with a grain of salt, "Saved from Siberia" and "Me — in the World Championship?" which are both make believe, all the rest, believe it or not, are true.

Besides Claire, I must take time out to thank my two editors, Ron Garber, who did a yeoman's job, and Phyllis Kantar, who hasn't let a mistake of mine pass by since year one.

Eddie Kantar
June 9, 1977

My Father's Son, the Bridge Teacher

Early in life I decided I would either have to work for a living or enjoy myself. Observation showed that very few people could combine both. I decided to enjoy myself. I became a bridge teacher.

I have been teaching bridge for the past 17 years; steadily for the past six or seven. I can just see Stoney wince as he reads this. He is not feeling sorry for me, mind you, but for the people I've been teaching.

You see, Stoney thinks I can barely follow suit. But that's not really an insult. Stoney thinks only five people in the world can play bridge, and he's not fully convinced about the other four.

Incidentally, Alvin Roth and Tobias Stone have thoroughly indoctrinated their followers that five-card majors are the only way to play. If I ever happen to get a decent result against a Roth-Stoner by opening a four-card major, he invariably takes my hand out of the board and he and his partner examine my four-card suit as though it were some kind of snake.

However, for all of Stone's conversation, Roth makes him look like a piker. In Toronto, when Marshall Miles and I played (and I use the term generously) on the same K. O. team with them, Roth would inspire confidence in Marshall and me by making a plane reservation home before each match.

I only mention this because I teach my classes to open four-card majors, if the hand calls for it, and I wanted the five-card majorites to know this before reading on. Four-card-major propaganda may be on their banned reading list.

Oh yes, I also teach them to count for long suits instead of short ones when originally evaluating their hands. I would estimate conservatively that this has cost me close to three years of my life in futile explanations. (Many of my ladies sneak Goren books into class.)

Once I mentioned that in order to give your partner a double raise you need at least four trumps and 13-16 points in support of partner's suit. Suddenly a women began leafing through her Goren book. She looked at the woman she came with, and with obvious relief, said, "He's going to be all right — he tells the truth!"

Now that I am in my declining years I have recklessly begun to teach limit raises. Live it up, and let the chips fall where they may.

I started out, naively enough, by teaching beginners. I should have realized immediately that I was not cut out for this. In one of my first classes I walked over to help someone play a hand. After a few tricks every single card in the dummy was good and there was no way, even for this lady, to lose another trick. I simply said, "Go over to the dummy and take the rest of the tricks." With that, I left to assist at another table. As I glanced back I saw the lady walking around the table to get over to the dummy!

At times they call me over to the table. "What should I play now?" the declarer usually asks me. I take a look and see six cards in everybody's hand. "What's trump?" I ask, stalling for time. "Hearts." "Do they have any left?" "One or two, but only little ones." "Are those clubs in dummy good?" "I don't remember, it's been a long time since they were played. Esther," she asks her right-hand opponent, "are those clubs in dummy good?" "How should I know? I'm not playing the hand." By this time I've sneaked a look at all of the hands. You wouldn't believe some of the endings!

Sometimes they come and tell me about a hand they played at home the night before. "I was playing with my husband," the story usually begins (she's clearly looking for sympathy, but she forgets I'm on *his* side), "and he bid three spades. What should I have done?"

"You mean he opened three spades?"

"No, I bid one heart, he gave me one spade, I gave him three clubs." (This is a very generous game.) "And he mentioned three spades. What should I have done?"

"Do you remember your hand?" I try.

"Oh yes, my hand. I had no spades — or maybe one — the queen, king, ten, ace, nine and an x in hearts — like you put on the board — the king of diamonds with some others, and the rest clubs, but it doesn't matter. Anyway, I said four hearts and he said we could have made three notrump. Was he right?"

"No," I say, hating myself. "You were right. You had an automatic four heart bid."

The last straw came up a few years ago when I was teaching the fifth lesson of a series for beginners. This particular lady came to class thinking it was the first lesson, and she just happened to sit South. I had a prepared hand on the table, open-faced, and was about to explain the bidding. I began by saying that South was the dealer and that with 14 points and a five-card spade suit — in beginning classes you give them at least five-card suits or they won't bid at all — the correct opening was one spade.

"Mr. Kantar," this woman said, raising her hand, "*which* spade should I bid?"

After a bit you get to recognize questions of this type. If you try to answer them you usually wind up wishing you *had* gone to work for a living. I parried. "Why don't you wait a bit and you'll see what the bidding means." She seemed satisfied, so I continued: "South opens one spade...." "Mr. Kantar, where should I put the spade that South opens?"

Well, I answered that question, and that is why I no longer teach "beginning" classes. I now call my classes "intermediate" and "advanced." The fact that the same people come does not disturb me.

In all of these classes I start out by giving a 20- to 40-minute lecture on the topic of the day and then call out prepared hands for distribution at the tables. Each player takes a suit, and I call off one suit at a time. Using this method I can teach any number of tables without trouble—provided everyone distributes the cards properly.

The fact that "eight" and "ace" sound so much alike has caused endless confusion—to say nothing of those students who forget to distribute the suit they are holding, to say nothing of the fact that somebody *always* winds up with too many or too few cards, to say nothing of the fact that almost no one bothers to count his cards, to say nothing of my mistakes as I call the cards. Otherwise it is an infallible system.

In one of my "beginning" classes (which I had been teaching for about five years) a truly memorable event occurred. Having called out the hands, I noticed that one lady had wound up with 20 cards and her partner six! True to their code of trusting me implicitly, it didn't seem to faze either of them.

The lady with the 20 cards was one of my better students; by that I mean she had decided to go all-out and count for long suits, regardless of what certain books said. She was trying to count up her hand, but her real problem was in trying to hold on to her cards. She needed a basket; they kept falling. Finally she got organized, and with her 6-8-4-2 distribution she came through admirably with a one heart opening. Next hand passed, and her partner was in a quandary.

This was an older woman, who had counted for short suits all her life, and she wasn't going to let a young upstart change her bidding habits. Relying on her years of experience, she realized that with her 0-1-3-2 distribution she had a truly magnificent hand. Why, in short suits alone she practically had an opening bid! Finally she called me over. "Mr. Kantar, Mr. Kantar!" she shouted hysterically. "I've never seen a hand like this before! What should I bid?" Had I been in a particularly fiendish mood I would have counted up her hand with her, but the sight of her partner trying valiantly to hold her cards sobered me and I finally revealed all. But it hurt.

Some women have been so overcome with my teaching that they can't wait to tell me how much they got out of one of the lessons. A little while back a lady came up to me after class and said that the lesson I had given the week before on redoubles had really helped her.

She proceeded to tell me about a recent hand. "My right-hand opponent opened one heart and I doubled. Next player passed, and my partner redoubled—just as you said, because she had more than ten points." "Redoubled?" I said. "Your partner can't redouble your double." "Oh," she said, "I knew there was something funny about the bidding."

Over the years, one tries not to repeat the same mistakes. The error I keep making is trying to teach them which card to lead, especially in partner's suit. I know and they know that they are going to lead the highest card, whatever I say, but they are very polite while I'm explaining.

One lady, however, couldn't stand it. As I was going through my spiel of why it is better to lead low from an honor, this woman stood up in the middle of the room and said, "I can't. They won't let me do it at my Woman's Club. I have to lead my highest." So what are you going to do about that?

If there is one thing a dedicated teacher likes to see it is progress. A clear indication of lesson application was hammered home to me after a class on card-combinations which included "Surrounding Plays." This is a term I learned from Arthur Robinson, which helps to illustrate this familiar type of play:

North
10 5 4

                                   East
                                   A J 9

East is on lead, and having the ten in dummy "surrounded" with the J-9, should lead the jack. This seemed simple enough. I had concocted a hand where East would eventually get the lead, and with a K-J-9 over a ten in dummy, was to lead the jack.

However, I overlooked something. At Trick 1, West led a small card in a different suit, and this was the dummy's holding in the suit led:

North
6 4 3

West   **East**
2   K 7 5

Dummy played low and East played the *seven*, thereby triumphantly "surrounding" the six-spot! I later analyzed the play and
decided the conflict between third-hand-high and the "surrounding" lesson was just too much. East had cracked under the pressure.

Incidentally, third-hand play is one of my favorite lessons because it gives me a chance to ask questions like this:

North
x x x

West   **East**
Q x x x x   J

South
A

I ask them (after sufficient explanation) to pretend that they
are West, defending a notrump contract. "Assume," I say, "you
lead a low card and your partner plays the jack, which loses to
declarer's ace. Who has the king?" (That, of course, is a pretty
tough one for the class, but I am ruthless.)

Aside from the few who think it is in the dummy, most of the
people who believe that false-carding amounts to cheating will
answer "East." The bright ones always say "South," but I once had
a lady who liked to play safe. Her answer was "Southeast."

In line with this theme, I was trying to get the point across of
unblocking for your partner in situations like this:

North
7 5 4

West   **East**
Q   K 2

I said: "Pretend you are East and that your partner leads the queen against notrump. Which card would you play?" Silence. "Come on," I urged, take a chance." Finally one brave soul said that she would play the king. "Really?" I teased. "Would you actually put your king on partner's queen?" "No," she finally admitted, "I wouldn't, but I think you would — you're so tricky!"

As I mentioned earlier I enjoy my work, and I even teach a few people to play. Take the lady who, as declarer, would never attack a suit in which she didn't have the ace and king. Finally I forced her (by wrenching the card from her hand) to lead up to a K-J combination in dummy. I carefully explained that it was simply a guess — if she thought the ace was on her left, to play the king, and if she thought it was on her right, to play the jack. I went through it again, then asked her which one she wanted to play from dummy, and to tell me what she was hoping for when she made her play.

After indescribable agony, she finally played the king. "What are you hoping for?" I asked. "I'm hoping they make a mistake," was the profound reply.

"The System" in Action

One of the main difficulties in playing so many conventions is that it puts an added mental strain on the partnership. Not only do you have to remember what you are playing, but you also have to remember the ramifications and minor changes you have adopted to fit your own bidding style.

Fortunately, my most frequent partner, Marshall Miles, and I seldom forget what we are playing. We never have more than three mental lapses a session — on a good day.

One "minor" misunderstanding stands out. Playing in the Nationals at Lexington, Kentucky, we arrived at a contract of seven clubs, with A-K-8 of clubs facing a void!

As no book that either Marshall or I have ever read described the proper play (for no losers) with this trump combination, our contract was not successful.

Since many players in Lexington were interested in exactly how we managed to get to this contract, I thought I would outline the bidding, and point out all the advanced nuances known only to those select few who can arrive at this type of contract.

Three meanings will be attached to each bid:

1. The systemic meaning: What the bid is supposed to mean.

2. The bidder's meaning: What the bidder thought the bid was supposed to mean.

3. The interpretation: What the partner of the bidder thought the bid meant.

Theoretically, in a good partnership these meanings should be one and the same. However, there have been times when there has been a slight difference of opinion even in the best partnerships.

Now for the hand. Marshall was South and dealer; I was North.

North
♠ A Q 5 4
♡ 5 4
◇ Q 10 8 7 6 5 3
♣ none

South
♠ K J 8 7 6
♡ A K 3
◇ A 4
♣ A K 8

THE BIDDING: ROUND 1

South: Two clubs.

Systemic meaning: A strong hand. (Artificial bid.)

Bidder's meaning: I have a strong hand.

Interpretation: All right, you have a strong hand.

North: Two diamonds.

Systemic meaning: A weak hand, or one that cannot be accurately limited. (Artificial response.)

Bidder's meaning: I know I'm supposed to have a weak hand but I really don't know what to respond, so I'll bide my time.

Interpretation: Probably a weak hand. (Notice how well we understand each other!

ROUND 2

South: Two notrump.

Systemic meaning: A balanced hand with 22-24 points.

Bidder's meaning: Same.

Interpretation: Same.

North: Four diamonds.

Systemic meaning: A specialized conventional bid asking opener to show a four-card minor if he has one.

Bidder's meaning: I should have bid three diamonds in the first place, so now I have to show my strength. I'll worry about my spades later.

Interpretation: Good! We have a chance to use our new convention. I hope he hasn't forgotten, and I hope he realizes that I haven't forgotten! He wants to know if I have a four-card minor.

ROUND 3

South: Four hearts.

Systemic meaning: A conventional response showing no four-card minor.

Bidder's meaning: I have no four-card minor. This convention sure is working smoothly! (Why does he look so serious? Is he worrying that I've forgotten our understanding? I remember, I remember!)

Interpretation: Wonderful! He fits my diamond suit and is showing me heart control. Looks like we are heading for a grand slam that the rest of the field may miss. (We got there, all right!)

North: Four spades.

Systemic meaning: From here on in the system gets a little foggy as we never had a chance to use our four diamond minor suit asking bid before.

Bidder's meaning: I think I'll show my ace of spades, and if it turns out that we have a spade fit, I can always say that I bid my spades. Sort of a two-way bid.

Interpretation: He asked for my four-card minor and I gave him a denial when I bid four hearts. He didn't bid either minor or sign off at four notrump, so he must be cue-bidding the ace or a void in spades. He must be terribly long in the minors and, with that master cue bid he just made, I can't let this hand play in less than seven. I must have all the right cards. I might shake him up a bit with my next bid, but what else can I do?

ROUND 4

South: Seven clubs.

Systemic meaning: A hand that should play in seven clubs.

Bidder's meaning: It's so nice to play with a partner who describes his hand so well! Wait till I tell them back home about this one. I can just see my partner's hand:

$$♠ — \quad ♡ x x \quad ◇ K Q x x x \quad ♣ Q J 10 x x x$$

(Please notice how clearly Marshall gauged my heart holding.)

Interpretation: Why, that sneaky devil. So it *was* a solid club suit all along. No need to worry, Marshall old boy — I got the word; I'm not going to pull it. Of course you don't know that I am void in clubs but your suit is certainly solid. I guess we must be in our best spot. (I just hope the clubs break.)

P.S. For those of you who are still there, the clubs did break! With the lucky 6-4 trump break, Marshall went down only five tricks. He later told me that good defense could have beaten him six, but he had played the hand very deceptively.

He also said that the opponents could not understand our bidding. (I had left the table after they took their third trick.) He also told me, gleefully, that they had let him make his eight of clubs by playing a fourth round of hearts. I nodded admiringly.

Vive la France!

One normally doesn't go to Europe on a honeymoon expecting to play bridge. But then again one doesn't always go on a honeymoon with a bridge player!

You see, I married a bridge player. She doesn't resent my going out to play bridge; she encourages me. She doesn't mind when I go into long trances in the middle of the day, figuring out a hand; she likes me all the more! Clearly, this is one of the strangest marriages of all time.

Anyway, this story begins and ends in Paris. Sounds pretty romantic, doesn't it? Here we are with about four days left to our trip having already visited every museum, plus the Eiffel Tower, taken a boat ride up the Seine, walked up and down the Champs Elysées a dozen times, and so forth and so on, à la all the tourists. In short, we were miserable. Why? We hadn't played bridge in about three weeks, and it was getting to both of us — that's why!

I decided to phone a few clubs. I would speak my best French and they would surely understand. After all, hadn't I majored in foreign languages? I would even say allo instead of hello.

Somehow, I gave myself away. I started speaking French and they answered in English. Already I was at a psychological disadvantage.

At first they were a little hesitant about our respective abilities. I started to shout: "I write articles . . . books . . . I can *play!*" I was drawing a crowd outside of the booth. All right, I was told, come over at nine o'clock and we'll try to work out a duplicate. It sounded a little fishy, but I was desperate. We went.

Somehow, the minute we walked in they knew we were "the Americans." One of the managers of the Elysées Club (go there if you are ever in Paris), Mr. Klotz, introduced himself and said they were trying to work up a team game.

It seems that they have these little games almost every night. Three teams-of-four play against one another in such a way that two matches go on simultaneously.

The first problem was that all players are chosen by the captains of the teams, and I wanted to make sure I played with Phyllis, who, at this point, was clutching her knees to stop the knocking. The second problem was that they weren't sure we could follow suit, and nobody wanted to be stuck with us. To encourage Phyllis a little, they told her that the French team had just won the European Championship in Warsaw, that all the members of the team play in this club, and maybe a couple of them might be in the team game. She turned purple-green.

They finally decided to let us play together, and the rest of them would choose up sides. Then the haggling started: Who would play with whom on whose team? I felt right at home; this was the type of action I was accustomed to. One of the players leaned over and whispered that we would all be playing but it would take another 45 minutes to choose teams—it happened that way every night and it wasn't because of us. I was even made an honorary captain. I immediately chose Klotz, because he knew the other players and he spoke English.

Sides were finally chosen. But what were the stakes? Nobody could tell me in English what I was playing for. Oh well, I still had my traveler's checks in case of a disaster.

We adjourned to a back room to play against Desrousseaux, a former world par-bridge champion and one of France's best, and his partner, Daniel Versini, who had just missed making the

French team this year, and who, if worst came to worst, could be a movie star if he did nothing but just stand there. Clearly, Phyllis was going to have a little trouble concentrating. I knew one thing—she would never double Versini even if she had him beat three tricks in her own hand!

The first hand was dealt and I suddenly realized I didn't know what I had. (French cards, of course!) All the jacks, queens and kings looked alike. I noticed Phyllis surreptitiously fishing for her glasses.

The game got started. Everyone was going to try to bid in English. Why wouldn't they ever let us practice our French? We knew the names of all the suits, and that they were all masculine. (We had asked someone on the Metro, just in case.)

The first two hands were a little unnerving. Phyllis led away from a king each time, letting Desrousseaux make two impossible part-scores. Then this:

North
♠ 7
♡ Q J 10 6
♢ K J 8 7
♣ Q 8 5 4

West
♠ Q 8
♡ 4 3
♢ A Q 10 6 4 3
♣ 10 3 2

East
♠ J 10 6 5 3
♡ 7 5 2
♢ 9 2
♣ K 9 6

South
♠ A K 9 4 2
♡ A K 9 8
♢ 5
♣ A J 7

Somehow they got to six hearts, and Phyllis led the ace of diamonds. At this point the hand is cold with any defense. I didn't help matters any by mentioning that an original trump lead, followed by a second trump upon winning the ace of diamonds, would have defeated the hand.

Something had to be done. Vulnerable against not, I picked up:

♠ A 10   ♡ A 9 6 4 2   ◊ K 10 7 4   ♣ 8 3

I opened one heart. We had to get a plus—all of those minuses were discouraging me. Phyl bid one notrump. I bid two diamonds. Now came three hearts! When this dummy came down I could see we were going to have to have a little discussion.

North
♠ 8 6 4
♡ Q 7 3
◊ Q 8 2
♣ A J 6 5

South
♠ A 10
♡ A 9 6 4 2
◊ K 10 7 4
♣ 8 3

A low club was led. Versini won with the queen and returned a spade to my ace. Desperate, I led a low club to the jack, which lost to the king. (Two kibitzers got up to leave.) Now I was forced in spades.

I tried the ace of hearts, which dropped the ten from Versini, then led a low heart to the queen and king. Why wasn't Versini thinking? He was just sitting there. Minutes passed. I asked to see the last trick. Versini's king wasn't the king, it was the jack. It was my lead. Do you think Versini knew who had the king?

I cashed my ace of clubs and ruffed a club, West discarding a spade. The stage was set for my first end-play in Paris. I would lead a diamond to the queen and then throw Desrousseaux in with the king of hearts and end-play him in diamonds, for down one.

I led a diamond to the queen. Versini won with the ace and returned a diamond. I finessed the ten. Desrousseaux made his
doubleton jack, cashed the king of hearts and produced another
spade. Down three. *All* the kibitzers left.

Amidst a growing silence we suffered another minus when I
failed to make four spades doubled, vulnerable, on a hand that
was cold via a mere dash of double-dummy technique. I began to
make a mental count of my remaining traveler's checks.

The stage was now set for the coup de grace. This came next:

North
♠ K Q J
♡ 8 3
◇ A K 7 6
♣ K J 9 3

West
♠ 10 7 6 4 2
♡ 10 9 4
◇ Q J 8 2
♣ 8

East
♠ 9
♡ A K J 6 2
◇ 10 5 4 3
♣ Q 7 6

South
♠ A 8 5 3
♡ Q 7 5
◇ 9
♣ A 10 5 4 2

Versini, South, wound up in four spades after Phyllis, East, had
overcalled with one heart. I led a heart, and Phyl played three
rounds of the suit, declarer discarding a diamond from dummy.

Two rounds of spades gave Versini something to think about.
After a few moments he cashed dummy's third spade, then led a
low club and finessed the ten! He now cashed his ace of spades,
discarding dummy's last small diamond, and ran his clubs. All I
could make was my ten of spades.

Versini had found the only winning line of play. Had he cashed
the king of clubs first, then finessed the ten, I would have ruffed

and thrown him in dummy with a diamond. He would then have no way of drawing my last trump.

When would this ever end? Mercifully, it was a short match and we did a little better in the second half. Financially, we broke even, because we did much better against the other team.

The next day Daniel told me that if Phyl had returned a club after winning the ace and king of hearts he could not have made the hand. I asked Phyl whether she would have shifted to a club if she had *known* it would defeat the contract. "Are you kidding?" answered the girl I had married.

I knew right then and there that we never could have beaten Daniel in four spades.

Saved from Siberia

John J. Underbid was a very conservative bidder; so conservative, in fact, that in a moment of super-timidity unusual even for him, he passed his partner's opening two-bid (strong variety)!

He had no excuse. He couldn't even say that he thought he was playing weak two-bids, because John J. never used weak two-bids. Perish the thought.

His partner, Raymond I. Neverpass, promptly hauled John J. down to the local Bridge Crime Courthouse, where the case was put on the calendar. Naturally, there was a long wait — 10 years, in fact — but at last John J. stood before the judge.

During the 10-year wait, John had switched bidding systems. He now used weak two-bids, weak notrumps and weak jump-overcalls. But the judge was not impressed. He surveyed the hand on which R. I. Neverpass had based his charge 10 years before, looked J. J. Underbid sternly in the eye, and thundered: "Were you guilty or not guilty of passing partner's opening two-bid on the night of March twenty-seventh, nineteen fifty-two, at the home of Raymond I. Neverpass?"

"Guilty," stammered John.

"What were the stakes?"

"We weren't playing for money, your honor."

"Irrelevant and immaterial," sneered the judge. "Do you really stand before this court and admit that you passed an opening two-bid? Why, this case is beneath the dignity of this court!"

John gulped.

"Have you atoned for this atrocity?"

"Yes, your honor. I now play all the weak conventions, and at high stakes. I have not passed a forcing bid for ten years! Why, just the other evening I raised a non-vulnerable three-bid to game when I was void in the trump suit!"

"You don't say," sneered the judge. "Kindly do not bring up hands that belong in the Court of Small Claims!"

"Sorry, your honor."

"All right, Underbid—you know your choice," said the judge.

John J. knew only too well. This was the moment he had been dreading. He could reaffirm his plea of guilty, pay the standard $3,000 fine, and be exiled to Gin Rummy and Canasta Land for 10 years, or he could try to make the hand the judge would give him to play. If he failed, he would never be permitted to play bridge again. Never!

Underbid glanced at his wife, Too Much, and at his sons, Hugh Bid and Hugh Overbid. Too Much was expecting again. Soon John J. might be able to have his own home game with no dirty court scandal lurking in the background to spoil everything. He had been meaning to teach his sons the game when they were three years old. He calculated how old they'd be when he returned from exile. He thought of other men and women who had been exiled. After their return they sorted their hands into runs and were always looking for wild cards. It was all too horrible to contemplate. "I'll play the hand!" John screamed.

"Very well," the judge said coldly. He handed John a paper napkin with four hands neatly pencilled thereon. "You have exactly ten minutes to make six hearts! The opening lead is the spade king."

John took the napkin and raced off to the Bridge Player's Inspiration Room, especially provided by the court for such emergencies. This was the layout:

North
- ♠ A 2
- ♡ 10 9 8 7
- ◇ A
- ♣ A J 10 4 3 2

West
- ♠ K Q J 9 8
- ♡ K 6 5
- ◇ 7 6 5
- ♣ 7 6

East
- ♠ 10 7 6 5
- ♡ 4
- ◇ Q 9 8 4
- ♣ K Q 9 8

South
- ♠ 4 3
- ♡ A Q J 3 2
- ◇ K J 10 3 2
- ♣ 5

John J. Underbid returned to the courtroom in exactly eight minutes and 30 seconds — with the correct solution!

Suppose you had been in his place? If your very future depended on making the six heart contract within 10 minutes, how would you play the hand?

Win the ace of spades, play the ace of clubs and trump a club with the heart jack. Enter dummy with a diamond and trump a club with the ace. Play the king of diamonds and discard dummy's last spade. Now play a small trump.

If West takes his king, win any return in dummy and ruff a club with the queen. South still has a small heart with which to enter dummy and pull West's remaining trumps. The clubs are now high. (If West returns a trump, win in dummy, trump a club, and trump a spade to enter dummy and pull West's remaining trump.)

If West ducks the first heart play, dummy wins, and the fourth club is trumped high. If West overtrumps, that is his last trick; and if he refuses, a trump is played and West can take no more than his king of hearts.

This coincided with the judge's official solution, and John J. Underbid walked out of the courtroom a free man. He went on to become a respected member of the community, and even had his own weekly team-of-four games with his three sons—his wife never played; she was Too Much—and never again set foot near the Bridge Crime Courthouse.

The Threepenny Opera

You've heard about the credibility gap, haven't you? This hand from the three-penny game at the Savoy Club in Los Angeles is sure to test it to the fullest. But first, the characters:

North: Fran Tsacnaris—Don't worry about pronouncing the name. She is a very competent player who works at the club and has learned to expect anything and everything.

East: Art Fletcher—A fine rubber-bridge player who struck gold in the pizza business.

South: Doc Freed—A plastic surgeon who has been known to mold something out of nothing, and conversely.

West: George Zahler—A Los Angeles Builder who frequently displays flashes of brilliance. George has the distinction of always being at the table when something happens.

ACT I—THE BIDDING

At first, you will only be allowed to see Zahler's hand in the West position. He is the dealer, and only Doc and "Zackamacka-frass" are vulnerable. Zahler holds:

♠ A K 9 2   ♡ —   ◇ Q J 10 4 2   ♣ K 9 5 4

The bidding proceeds:

West	North	East	South
1 ◇	Pass	1 ♡	2 ♣
Double	Pass	Pass	2 ♠
Double	Pass	Pass	Pass

So the Doc is playing the hand in two spades doubled, and the opponents exchange hands while Zahler considers his lead. He finally decides on the queen of diamonds, and the dummy comes down:

North
♠ Q J 8 7
♡ A 2
◇ 6 3
♣ A Q 8 3 2

West
♠ A K 9 2
♡ none
◇ Q J 10 4 2
♣ K 9 5 4

This is one of the most disturbing dummies ever to hit the table at the Savoy. It is so disturbing, in fact, that Fletcher, in the East chair, stands up to take a better look, mentally calculating his loss in terms of pizza parlors.

ACT II — THE PLAY

After all of the commotion has subsided, the play begins. Fletcher plays the nine of diamonds at trick one, and the queen holds. Before looking at all four hands, what would you play at trick two from the West position?

North
♠ Q J 8 7
♡ A 2
◇ 6 3
♣ A Q 8 3 2

West
♠ A K 9 2
♡ none
◇ Q J 10 4 2
♣ K 9 5 4

East
♠ 3
♡ K Q 8 7 6 5
◇ K 9
♣ J 10 7 6

South
♠ 10 6 5 4
♡ J 10 9 4 3
◇ A 8 7 5
♣ none

Admit it. You thought that the dummy was really declarer's hand, didn't you? It wasn't. It was the real dummy!

The Doc was out molding again—this time, something out of nothing. Zahler, in the midst of all the excitement, decided to give his partner a club ruff! (Ace-king and a spade would have been much better.)

The Doc finessed the queen and cashed the ace of clubs, discarding hearts, and ruffed a club. Next came the ace of diamonds and a diamond ruff, for five tricks; a club ruff followed for six, and a diamond ruff for seven.

At this point, the dummy has the queen-jack of spades doubleton, two hearts and the last club. The Doc has the doubleton ten of spades and three hearts, with the lead in the dummy.

If Doc ruffs the fifth club with the ten of spades, he must make the hand. The Doc plays the ace of hearts! Zahler ruffs, draws trumps, and takes the balance, for down one!

Now, let me tell you about the next deal, which was really exciting . . .

The First Board*

Haven't you ever wondered how or why certain people keep winning most of the bridge tournaments? We know that we can play better, and we simply can't pin *all* the blame on our partners even if they deserve it. Could it possibly be that these perennial winners know something that we don't?

I have a hunch that these winners understand the philosophy of the "first board." The idea behind this philosophy is somehow to undermine the confidence of either one or preferably both opponents on the first board, and before they can regain equilibrium, to mow them down on the second.

All well and good, but how do you go about this?

Before I discuss some new artifices, we should review two standard gimmicks. Without these no one can ever be a regular winner.

The first and most often employed is the "make them feel bad" gimmick. After the hand is over and you have carefully hacked up another hand in two spades and the opponents are sitting up in their chairs, you mention the fact that all along they were cold for three hearts. Whether either one of them had enough to get into the bidding is completely irrelevant. They were cold for three

*This article is to be taken with a large grain of salt.

25

hearts and you must let them know about it. Their smiles of triumph will fade, and you can be sure they will be in the bidding on the next hand, whatever they have.

The second standard maneuver is not to let a bad play by the enemy get away unnoticed. However, the trick is to time the comment properly and to deliver it in the proper tone of voice.

Let's say that West has let you make a game contract by leading the wrong suit near the end of a rather difficult hand. You say nothing. You must wait until the players have pulled out their cards from the next board. Then, in an aside to East that West is "not supposed" to hear you very casually mention the fact that a diamond lead by West, instead of the spade he choose, would have beaten you. Obviously, this sets up a fine mood (for you) on the second board.

I realize that I am wasting time by repeating these standard ploys but I have been working on this subject for quite a while. Now I would like to present three new types. The first is called "Faking a Ruff," and it goes something like this:

North
- ♠ A 6 4
- ♡ A Q 4 3
- ◇ Q 6 4
- ♣ A 5 2

West
- ♠ 3
- ♡ 10 9 8 7
- ◇ K 10 9 8
- ♣ 10 6 4 3

East
- ♠ J 2
- ♡ K J 6
- ◇ A 5 3 2
- ♣ J 9 8 7

South
- ♠ K Q 10 9 8 7 5
- ♡ 5 2
- ◇ J 7
- ♣ K Q

You become declarer at four spades, and West leads the ten of hearts. Being a gambler at heart, you play the queen, and when this loses to the king you utter a silent prayer that East will not find the diamond shift.

East goes into a long trance and finally produces the deuce of diamonds. You play the seven and West wins with the king. West now returns the ten of diamonds. You play low from dummy and East plays the ace, which you trump. Yes, I know you are revoking, but let me finish.

At this point you must make sure that you are considering your next play very seriously. Do not look up to see what is happening. I will tell you.

East is having a mini-stroke. You see, he thinks his partner has returned the ten of diamonds, holding the jack! West, on the other hand, thinks that his partner must have the jack of diamonds hidden behind another card. Baleful looks are flashing across the table.

East will be the first to speak. "Have we changed our signalling system recently—like in the past five seconds, partner?" West will ignore this and slowly and deliberately ask his partner to please count his cards. East will be on the verge of an eruption (these plays should really be saved for the mixed pairs, come to think of it) when you innocently come to the rescue.

"Gosh!" you gasp. "Here's that jack of diamonds—it was mixed up in my hearts."

The over-all effect is just beautiful! First, you have made it clear to the opponents that they don't trust each other. Second, each will inwardly hate the other for alerting you to your stupid revoke. They should be easy pickings on the next board.

This ploy has interesting ramifications. Just the other day I tried it in a rubber game—and even the kibitzers stood up. Basically, the situation was this:

$$\begin{array}{c}
\textbf{North} \\
\diamond \ \text{J 4 3 2}
\end{array}$$

West		**East**
◇ 9 8 7		◇ A Q 6 5

$$\begin{array}{c}
\textbf{South} \\
\diamond \ \text{K 10}
\end{array}$$

You are playing a spade contract, and West leads the diamond nine. You duck in dummy and East elects to play the six. You win with the ten. Then West gets the lead in another side suit and plays the eight of diamonds. This time East puts up the ace, and naturally, you trump.

Right here, East angrily announces to the kibitzers that West's proper lead from K-9-8-7 was the seven, not the nine. The kibitzers snicker. They knew that. West is livid. He's the one who is being laughed at — when his partner was (and is) the biggest idiot of all time! Holding the A-K-Q of diamonds, East let you win Trick 1 with the ten! Unprintable yelling goes back and forward across the table. You let this go on for a little time before you produce the diamond king — with due apologies, of course.

For those readers who are eager to know the combinations (besides those already given) that are most likely to produce blood, I suggest as a starter:

	North Q 5 4	
West 10 9 8 7		East K 6 3 2
	South A J	

West leads the ten and you win with the jack. West gets in again and leads the nine. East plays low again, and you ruff. Remember, don't play anything — just ruff and wait. The rest will take care of itself. I promise you.

Next:

	North J 6 5	
West 9 3		East A K 8 4 2
	South Q 10 7	

West leads the nine, and you drop the queen under the king. East plays the ace, and you ruff . . .

If these fail to produce the desired results, do not give up. "The Advance Claim Gambit" may be lurking around the corner—a sure winner:

North
♠ A Q 7 5
♡ A Q 2
◇ J 9 8 6
♣ 3 2

West
♠ 8 6
♡ 9 7 4
◇ K 5 3
♣ K 9 7 6 4

East
♠ 9 3
♡ K 8 6 5
◇ A 10 7
♣ Q 10 8 5

South
♠ K J 10 4 2
♡ J 10 3
◇ Q 4 2
♣ A J

This time you are in three spades and West leads the nine of hearts. You play the queen, and East wins and shifts to a low club. You take this, draw two rounds of trumps, strip the hearts and casually lay your hand on the table announcing that you have to lose two diamonds and a club—making three. You must carefully refrain from actually leading the club and making the forced diamond return obvious.

At this point one of two things will happen.

1. Both opponents will keep their cards up, and sooner or later one will ask, "How are you going to play that diamond suit?"

You look at him disdainfully and say, "I thought anybody would be able to see that baby throw-in play. I am going to lead a club and force you to play diamonds to me. Can't you see it?" you should repeat. Whoever asked now feels like the village idiot and should be mush on the next board.

2. The more likely possibility, however, when you spread your hand, is that at least one opponent will expose his cards from force of habit. Both opponents will examine your hand carefully, and one is bound to blurt out, "Just how are you going to handle that diamond suit?"

You look at the defender's exposed hand and say, "Well, now that I can see who has the ten of diamonds, I will . . ." An uproar will ensue; the director will be summoned; but you are safe. All you have to do is lead your club as you intended all along. It ought to take them at least one board to regain composure.

Although it is close to impossible that either of these ploys will go wrong, you still have the coup de grace at your disposal, namely, "The Hidden Ball Trick":

                         North
                         ♠ 9 3 2
                         ♡ A Q
                         ◇ K Q J 10
                         ♣ K Q J 5

West   East
♠ J 5 4   ♠ 10 8 7 6
♡ 10 8 6 2   ♡ 9 7 5 4
◇ A 6   ◇ 9 8 7
♣ 10 8 6 4   ♣ A 9
                         South
                         ♠ A K Q
                         ♡ K J 3
                         ◇ 5 4 3 2
                         ♣ 7 3 2

This time you are playing three notrump. Your grandmother can make five in her sleep, but you battle on.

West leads the deuce of hearts and you win with the queen, playing the three from your hand. East signals with the seven. You lead the king of diamonds. West wins with the ace and returns a low heart. This time you play the king under the ace, saving the jack.

Now you play a couple of rounds of diamonds and West discards a heart. After all, if you don't have any more hearts, West doesn't need to save both hearts, and a club or a spade discard could be costly.

The moment West discards a heart, East knows that West cannot have the jack for he would be throwing good tricks away. So, actually, they are both reasoning quite well. We will definitely have to do something about that!

You now lead the king of clubs from dummy. East wins with the ace and, knowing the futility of a heart return, tries a spade.

At this point you are solid. Your play is marked and you move in for the kill. You casually hide the jack of hearts behind one of your other cards and hold your hand out for everyone to see, at the same time murmuring that someone must have forgotten to cash good hearts.

East, of course, will be furious because West pitched a heart, holding the jack, and will demand to be told how West could have been such an idiot. West will snarl "What jack?" and upbraid East for not even knowing that he—*East!*—had that card.

Remember, do not laugh! Let them alone. The longer they keep it up, the better your prospects become. Of course they'll finally grab your cards and locate the elusive heart jack, but the damage has been done to them: each is secretly aware that he doesn't really trust the other as far as he can throw the water cooler.

So—you were wondering how some people win tournaments? Shame on you. Now go out there and dazzle 'em with your footwork! *But don't forget to do it on the first board!*

The World's Greatest Bridge Bids

(Some of the Worst As Well As a Few of the Best)

YOU MUST FOLLOW SUIT!!!

It all happened a few years ago in the Life Masters Women's Pairs in Miami Beach. You may not believe this but there were witnesses.

North-South vul.

Dealer East

```
                    North
                    ♠ 9 5 4 2
                    ♡ J 10 9 8 5
                    ◇ 4
                    ♣ K 9 8

West                                        East
♠ 10                                        ♠ 8 7 6
♡ A Q 6 4                                   ♡ K 7 3 2
◇ 9 5 3                                     ◇ K 8
♣ A J 7 6 3                                 ♣ Q 10 4 2

                    South
                    ♠ A K Q J 3
                    ♡ None
                    ◇ A Q J 10 7 6 2
                    ♣ 5
```

The bidding: (If you excuse the expression)

East	South	West	North
Pass	2♣	2♠!	Pass
Pass	3◇	Pass	3♡
Pass	3♣!!	Pass	3♡
Pass	3♠	Pass	4♣
Pass	4◇	Pass	5◇
All pass			

Opening lead: 10 ♠

I'd hate to be the first to say that this could only happen in a Women's Pair event, but I will.

West, Isa Alcone of New York, decided to scramble things up a bit with a spade psychic. South, in a daze, made a crazy insufficient bid at the three level which was condoned by West's pass. North seized the opportunity to rebid her five card suit at the three level . . . twice!

But on to the play. South grabbed the spade opening and immediately plunked down the ace and ten of diamonds to East's king, West high-lowing in trumps to show a strong desire (more like a lust) to ruff something.

East obliged with a spade return which West duly ruffed. "Just a moment," said declarer, "you must play a spade, you bid them!"

When West made no motion to comply, declarer insisted: "you must follow suit." When West still refused, declarer finally called (screamed to be exact) for the director. Many directors came. However, not one of them could find a spade in the West hand. West cashed the ace of clubs and the contract was down one.

WHY'D YOU LEAVE ME IN DIAMONDS?

Have you ever had the ghastly experience of holding a mile-long suit playing with an inexperienced partner who has a long suit or two of his own and becomes defiant as you begin bidding and rebidding and re-rebidding your suit?

North-South vul.
Dealer South

North
♠ 7
♡ Q 4
◇ 10 2
♣ A K Q J 7 5 3 2

West   **East**
♠ K 9 8 5   ♠ J 6 3
♡ J 10 9 8 7   ♡ K 6 5 2
◇ 5   ◇ K J 9 8
♣ 10 9 4   ♣ 8 6

South
♠ A Q 10 4 2
♡ A 3
◇ A Q 7 6 4 3
♣ None

South	West	North	East
1 ◇	1 ♡ !	2 ♣	2 ♡
3 ♠	Pass	4 ♣	Pass
4 ◇	Pass	5 ♣	Pass
5 ◇	Pass	Pass!!	Double
Pass	Pass	Pass!!!	

Opening lead: J ♡

The bidding requires a little comment. I was North, playing in a tournament with a rather weak partner. West was angry, very angry, about the last hand, and was just bidding to try to make up for a previous error.

At the time I was trying to figure out just how high I was going to have to bid those clubs to get my partner to pass. From the sound of his voice, I knew that six would not be nearly enough. (Six clubs makes, by the way.)

Incidentally, my partner should have rebid four spades rather than four diamonds to show me his six-five hand. But if he were that smart, he would have been smart enough to let me play in clubs. My bidding probably wasn't so hot either. I think an original jump to three clubs, followed by club rebids is the best way to describe this type of hand. Now for the play.

The jack of hearts was covered by the queen, king and ace, and my partner started caressing my clubs, counting them, and shaking his head in disbelief.

The clubs stretched from one end of the table to the other.

I had purposely spread them out a bit extra, enraged that I couldn't play this hand in clubs.

After my partner counted my clubs two more times, he played the ace of spades and ruffed a spade on the table. Now came a high club upon which he discarded a heart. He then recounted my remaining clubs as West began to smoulder.

A second club was cashed, a spade discarded, and my partner took time out to—guess what. West could stand it no longer. "You had eight clubs in the dummy originally," he said. "You have played them twice. I have one left and my partner doesn't have any."

This was the position:

North
- ♠ none
- ♡ 4
- ◊ 10
- ♣ Q J 7 5 3 2

West
- ♠ K 9
- ♡ 10 9 8 7
- ◊ 5
- ♣ 10

East
- ♠ J
- ♡ 6 5 2
- ◊ K J 9 8
- ♣ none

South
- ♠ Q 10
- ♡ none
- ◊ A Q 7 6 4 3
- ♣ none

If my partner plays a third club and East ruffs, my partner can overruff, lead the queen of spades and actually make the hand. On the other hand, if East discards the jack of spades, the hand can never be made.

Suffice it to say that East did not discard the jack of spades and my partner did not make the hand.

The crowning blow came as we were leaving the table. I heard my partner mutter, "nine, I mean eight, clubs and he leaves me play the hand in diamonds."

"THE WORLD'S GREATEST BID"

Have you ever wondered what it would feel like to make the world's greatest bid? Erik Paulsen, nationally recognized expert, had that feeling recently. This was the hand that inspired "the world's greatest bid."

Both sides vul.
Dealer East

```
                    North (Paulsen)
                    ♠ K J 9 8 5 4 3
                    ♡ A K 10 6 5 4
                    ◇ None
                    ♣ None
   West                                    East
   ♠ A                                     ♠ None
   ♡ Q 2                                   ♡ J 9 8 7
   ◇ J 7 6 5 4 3                           ◇ Q 10 2
   ♣ 8 6 5 2                               ♣ A K J 9 4 3
                    South
                    ♠ Q 10 7 6 2
                    ♡ 3
                    ◇ A K 9 8
                    ♣ Q 10 7
```

The bidding:

East	South	West	North
1♣	1♠	2♣	5 NT
Pass	6♠	Double	7♠ *
Pass	Pass	Double	Pass
Pass	Pass		

***World's greatest bid**

Opening lead: A♠ (before it got away)

This bidding sequence is going to take a little bit of explaining, as do all genius inspired sequences. Keep in mind that this hand is from a duplicate bridge tournament where all tables eventually will be playing this same hand.

Paulsen's original jump to 5NT was the Grand Slam Force asking partner about the quality of his spade suit. The response of six spades was supposed to show one of the top two honors but deny two of the top three. In other words, from Paulsen's point of view, South had the ace of spades. South thought he was showing bad spades by bidding six spades. Of such confusions come great stories.

So, when Paulsen heard the response of six spades, he "knew" seven spades must be cold! As was mentioned before, this was a tournament hand so Paulsen had to do some fast calculating when West doubled.

Assuming seven spades is cold, North-South are entitled to a plus score of at least 2210. Passing six spades doubled making seven is only 1860, so clearly that can't be right. Paulsen now calculated how much he would make if he redoubled six spades and made seven. That would come to 2420, more than seven spades making seven.

So why didn't Erik simply redouble six spades? Because he is a genius! He figured that at the other tables, seven spades would be doubled! Seven spades doubled making seven is 2470, more than six spades redoubled making seven.

What else could he do? He couldn't settle for a mere 2420 when "all" the other tables would be garnering 2470. He clearly made the only logical call considering the circumstances. If you don't agree or you wish to ask him why he didn't redouble seven spades, you might speak to him about it . . . from a distance.

5 VS. 4

One of my favorite people was the late John Levinson, originally from Chicago, who also played golf professionally.

There was trouble with John right from the beginning. I like to play four card majors and John was wedded to five card majors.

In spite of this unalterable breach, we decided to play in the Blue Ribbon Pairs a couple of years ago when it was held in Phoenix.

Obviously someone had to give in and in the end (five minutes before game time) it was John, but he said he wouldn't be responsible for anything that happened if, God forbid, he should open with a four card major.

He also said he could not under any circumstances get himself to open one heart holding four hearts and five diamonds. He just couldn't. "Don't worry, John," I said, "it all works fine if you open one heart and rebid your diamonds."

"How is it going to work out fine," he asked, "when you have two hearts and three diamonds and take me back to hearts? How will you know to leave me in diamonds when we could be missing a 5-2 heart fit?"

"Don't worry about it, John, I never get dealt two hearts and three diamonds."

So we started to play and everything was going along just fine until John picked up four hearts and five diamonds and that $&%†@ opened one diamond. It turned out that I had four hearts to the queen and responded one no trump thinking that John couldn't have four hearts unless he was strong enough to reverse in which case he would bid them away. I didn't relish getting raised with three card support.

So we played one no trump down one when three hearts was ice cold. There were plenty of looks but nothing was said. Then this hand came along:

Neither side vul.
Dealer South

North (me)
♠ A Q J 3 2
♡ 9 3
◇ 10 9 4
♣ 10 4 3

West
♠ 9 8 7 6
♡ A K 8 7
◇ K 5 3
♣ A 2

East
♠ K 10 5 4
♡ 10 6 5
◇ J 6
♣ Q J 9 7

South (John)
♠ None
♡ Q J 4 2
◇ A Q 8 7 2
♣ K 8 6 5

Little did I know at the time what self-torture John was going through when he finally, grudgingly, opened the South hand with one heart.

I responded one spade and John dutifully bid two diamonds wondering what tragedy was about to befall him.

Normally I would pass two diamonds with the North hand, but knowing how John felt about such things, remembering the other hand quite vividly, and realizing we still had two more sessions to play in this event (somehow we were leading), I took John back to two hearts to "preserve partnership unity and morale."

Well, after everyone passed and John took one look at the dummy, I knew what had happened. He had tried to please me and I had tried to please him, and we had both gone against our best instincts. When the smoke cleared, John was down three tricks and shaking his head.

I just want to tell all of you that John Levinson and I resolved our problems with four and five card major suit openings once and for all. He opens one diamond, I open one heart, and we decided not to play together any more.

The bridge world will miss John Levinson.

The next hand is an outright steal from the British Bridge Magazine. It appeared in an article by the Scottish player-humorist, Albert Benjamin. Let him tell it.

Neither side vul.
Dealer South

```
                        North
                        ♠ K 5 4
                        ♡ J 6 3
                        ◇ K Q 10 5 4
                        ♣ 10 6

        West                              East
        ♠ A 9 2                           ♠ Q J
        ♡ K Q 10                          ♡ 9 8 7 5 4 2
        ◇ J 9 8 7                         ◇ 3 2
        ♣ 8 5 2                           ♣ 9 7 4

                        South
                        ♠ 10 8 7 6 3
                        ♡ A
                        ◇ A 6
                        ♣ A K Q J 3
```

South	West	North	East
1♠	Pass	2◇	Pass
3♣	Pass	3♠	Pass
4◇	Pass	4♠	Pass
5♣*	Pass	6♠**	All Pass

*How good are your spades?
**Not very good, how good are yours?
Opening lead: K ♡

I suffered the humiliation many years ago at the hands of Graham Matthieson and Ewart Kempson of not defeating six hearts redoubled although my partner and I jointly held the K Q J x x of trumps!

I am, therefore, pleased to report that this record has been broken by a pair of Scottish international players who allowed a small slam to be made against them although their combined trump holding was A Q J 9 2!

Almost incredibly South reached six spades and West led the king of hearts. South won and rather cleverly cashed the ace of diamonds before leading a low trump towards dummy. West was taking no chance of his heart winner disappearing on a diamond. He smartly stepped up with the ace of spades crashing his partner's jack. The queen of hearts was trumped and a spade to the king snatched the queen and South's ten picked up the nine. South claimed the balance.

East did not forget to point out that the two of diamonds did not appear when South played the ace, and if South's diamond ace really was a singleton, he, East, would have started with 6 3 2 and would never have played the three.

This logic, alas, fell on deaf ears. West had already committed suicide.

This hand received considerable press because I was playing with Jonathan Cansino, the British expert par excellence, in the Life Master's Pairs in Denver.

North-South vul.
Dealer South

                              North
                              ♠ A
                              ♡ K 9
                              ◇ A 10 9 8 7 6
                              ♣ A Q 3 2

    West (Cansino)   East
    ♠ K Q J 9 8 7 6 5   ♠ 10 4
    ♡ 2   ♡ Q 7 6 5
    ◇ J 4   ◇ K Q 3
    ♣ 8 5   ♣ K J 7 6

                              South
                              ♠ 3 2
                              ♡ A J 10 8 4 3
                              ◇ 5 2
                              ♣ 10 9 4

The bidding:

South	West	North	East
Pass	4♠	5◇	Double
5♡	Pass	Pass	Double
Pass	Pass	Pass	

Opening lead: K ♠

The problem arose when South bid five hearts. He was in doubt about what to do and when he finally did bid, it sounded to Jonathan as if he had bid five notrump! So there we were, Cansino defending five notrump doubled, while I am trying to defeat five hearts doubled.

After winning the first trick, declarer played ace and a diamond to my queen. (To legitimately defeat this contract I must unblock a diamond honor under the ace, allowing Jonathan to win the second diamond and play a club. In view of what Jonathan thought the contract was, this defense seems highly unlikely.)

I tranced for some time before deciding to return my last spade. When Jonathan saw that I had another spade, he sat up in his chair mumbling something about "what took you so bloody long" as he prepared to run his seven spades.

Dummy ruffed the spade with the nine of hearts and played the king of hearts simultaneously with Jonathan's next spade. Declarer thought trumps had broken badly and Cansino thought it odd declarer should discard the king of hearts on his "winning" spade.

Declarer decided to get back to his hand, ruffing a diamond as Cansino played yet another spade. These plays were all happening so close together it was impossible for me to tell what was going on.

Finally, when declarer played the ace of hearts on Cansino's fourth spade, it became apparent to everyone but Jonathan what had happened. Jonathan still had four more good spades to take, and by God he was going to.

The director was called over, the revoke rule enforced, and declarer was awarded five hearts doubled with an overtrick.

Poor Jonathan—thought he had seven good spades to run and all he wound up with was one revoke and a bottom board.

Speaking of eight card suits, I couldn't resist having a little fun in one of my classes with one. I was giving a lesson on entries and I have this trick hand that nobody in my previous classes had ever figured out. I decided to slip it in again just to see what would happen. It was wild.

Neither side vul.
Dealer East

North
♠ 8 3
♡ J 10 7
◇ 10 8 6
♣ A K J 10 5

West
♠ 10 9 4
♡ Q 9 8 4
◇ 2
♣ 9 8 7 6 4

East
♠ none
♡ 6 5 2
◇ K Q J 9 7 5 4
♣ Q 3 2

South
♠ A K Q J 7 6 5 2
♡ A K 3
◇ A 3
♣ none

East	South	West	North
3◇	6♠	Pass	Pass
Pass			

Opening lead: 2 ◇

We don't waste time on the bidding in my classes. The play's
the thing, you know. Do you see how to make six spades with a
diamond lead. If you do, don't come to my classes, you're too
smart.

The trick, of course, is to get to dummy's clubs without crawl-
ing under the table. The way to do this is to win the diamond
opening, cash two high spades and then exit with the deuce of
spades to West's higher spade. West must play either a heart or a
club and there you are in dummy.

Although I have a firm rule never to watch my students play
a hand (when they see me watching—it makes them nervous), I
broke my rule on this one hand and watched the play at three different tables.

At table I declarer ducked the diamond opening altogether. East then shifted to a heart but declarer still had to lose a heart. Down one.

At table II declarer cleverly won the diamond opening and then sneakily led a low spade at trick two. West courageously went up with the nine (second hand low is a hard maxim to overcome, you know) and then returned a heart. Declarer now made the hand thinking she was a genius.

At table III declarer won the diamond opening and immediately played the ace of clubs from dummy. (Clearly the best play if the defenders will let you get away with it.) Everyone followed. So she played the king of clubs and discarded her losing heart to make seven.

"What the problem?" she asked. I decided to stop watching.

Short, Anyway

When I asked Jeff Rubens in Vancouver if he wanted an article on the tournament, he answered, "Only if it is short and funny." Well. the first part of the request was easy.

In order to appreciate the following deal you must be aware of the prelude. I was playing with Bob Hamman in the Men's Team, and before the event I corralled him into taking a walk to the zoo in beautiful Stanley Park.

On the way the discussion turned to bridge, and for the umpteenth time he expounded his theories of being a practical player at the bridge table, bringing up hands from years ago where I had failed to heed this advice. I nodded. Then he mentioned a few hands that he had bid and played recently with the practical view in mind. I nodded. Then he told me about various other experts who would be getting much better results if they were a bit more practical. I nodded. After this two-sided conversation we sat down to do battle.

Our first opponents, seeing us play together for the first time in many a moon, asked us how come we were a partnership again. Hamman replied, "We both lost bets."

The deal in question was not the first we played in the event. It was the second. First, I will give you my hand as a problem.

You are sitting North, vulnerable against not, when your partner deals and passes and your righthand opponent opens three
diamonds. This is your hand:

♠ A Q J 9   ♡ Q   ◇ A 9 2   ♣ K Q J 9 8

What would you bid?

What was the practical bid, I asked myself? None came to mind,
so I bid what I thought was right, three notrump. This was passed
on my left; and after a lengthy pause Hamman bid four hearts,
just what I wanted to hear. This was passed around to my left-
hand opponent, who doubled. The bidding then came back to me:

South	West	North	East
Hamman		*Me*	
Pass	3 ◇	3 NT	Pass
4 ♡	Pass	Pass	Double
Pass	Pass	?	

I knew that Bob had six hearts, but why didn't he open a weak-
two? Obviously his hearts weren't that good, or, perhaps, he had a
heart-club two-suiter with five cards in each suit, or, perhaps, six
hearts and four spades. In any case, I convinced myself that four
hearts doubled was not the right contract. Now what was I to do—
in a practical vein, of course?

I reasoned that in this event, with board-a-match scoring, a redouble by me would surely be for takeout—as simply passing and
making four hearts doubled would insure a win on the board. I
made a rescue redouble. Everyone passed.

North
♠ A Q J 9
♡ Q
♢ A 9 2
♣ K Q J 9 8

South
♠ 4 3
♡ K 10 7 6 5 4
♢ Q
♣ A 10 5 3

Opening lead: J ♢

Before describing the intricacies of the play, I think it only fair that you know a bit more about the personality of lovable Bob. When he used to live in Los Angeles he played a tremendous amount of rubber bridge. And he was a winner. A big winner. But that wasn't all. He used to needle his opponents after he beat them. You would think that this combination of losing money while getting insulted would make them look for another game. No. Actually, the reverse took place. Everyone wanted to play in Hamman's game. The revenge motive.

Once a theoretical question was posed at the club. "If you were playing in a pivot game with Hamman, would you rather win $30 and see Hamman win $50, or lose $30 while seeing Hamman lose $50?" Never was there such unanimity of opinion. To a man, everyone would rather have lost the $30. . . . Now for the play.

Bob got off to a fast start by winning the opening diamond lead with the queen as East signalled with the eight. A low heart went to the queen and East's ace; a club came back.

The problem, as Hamman saw it, was to make the hand in case East had four or even five trumps to the A-J-9. Accordingly, he won the king of clubs in dummy and played a second club. West ruffed!

West now returned the king of diamonds to dummy's ace, as East completed the echo and Hamman discarded his losing spade.

Next came the ace and queen of spades, covered by the king and ruffed by Bob as West played the ten.

At this point, Hamman reasoned, if East started with four hearts to the ace-jack East was a dead duck. Dummy could be entered with a club, a club discarded on the jack of spades, and the nine of spades ruffed in the closed hand, leaving Bob with K-10-7 of hearts. He could now exit with a low heart and take the last two tricks.

There were two advantages to this line of play. First, the kibitzrs and I would both be impressed, and second he would not have to explain why he didn't retreat to five clubs as I had asked.

Confidently Bob led a third club. West ruffed! East still had to make his jack of hearts, and we were down one redoubled on a hand that was cold for five. Trumps had broken 3-3 all along.

Of course a practical player like Bob would never allow for West's ten of spades to be an honest card, in which case West would have started with 2-3-7-1 distribution. In any case, I heard practical Bob mutter after the hand was over, "Three trumps and a singleton club, and he leads a diamond!"

My last hand deals with a new technique conceived by Alan Sontag, playing with Cliff Russell in the same event. I call it "weak suit dummy concealment."

This was the entire deal:

Both sides vul.
Dealer South

North *(the magician)*
♠ A Q 4
♡ A K 9 8
◇ Q 6 5
♣ 10 6 2

West
♠ 9 6 2
♡ 10 7 4 2
◇ 10 7
♣ Q 9 7 3

East
♠ 7 3
♡ Q 5
◇ 9 4 3 2
♣ A J 8 5 4

South
♠ K J 10 8 5
♡ J 6 3
◇ A K J 8
♣ K

South	West	North	East
Russell		*Sontag*	
1♠	Pass	2♣!	Pass
2◇	Pass	2♡	Pass
2 NT	Pass	3 NT	(All Pass)

Rather than pervert his hand and show spade support, Sontag opted to steal the board at three notrump. After all, he had bid clubs, hadn't he?

West was so impressed that he led the deuce of hearts. Now Sontag began to have qualms about showing this dummy. He decided to conceal his club weakness temporarily, by placing the ace-queen of spades on his clubs and thus putting down this respectable dummy:

♠4 ♡A K 9 8 ◇Q 6 5 ♣A Q 10 6 2

Surely his bidding was now impeccable. There was only one catch—nobody at the table realized what had happened!

While all the other declarers in the room were agonizing over the management of the heart suit in a spade contract, Russell, without a care in the world, played low from dummy at trick one; East won the queen.

East now studied the dummy, presumably not noticing the duplication of strength in the club department. Sontag couldn't stand it any longer. He put his high spades where they belonged, leaving Russell with no club stopper—where he once thought that clubs was his best suit!

East, now grasping the position completely, shifted to a *low* club. Russell guessed to play his king and took the rest of the tricks.

Well, the article was short.

Ceci and Me

I met Ceci three months ago* and life has just not been the same, nor will it probably ever be.

Aside from everything else, Ceci adores playing bridge almost as much as she adores her cuddly Maltese, Minny, who kibitzes our games regularly with a lapside view. Throw in the sun (Ceci is an avid sunworshipper) and you will begin to get the idea of where I fit into the picture. At the moment I am a distant fourth and losing ground rapidly.

The only way I can possibly make it to third is to pick up some master points for Ceci. You see winning isn't the only thing to Ceci, it is everything. Ask her how many points she has and she will answer, "Oh, who keeps track?—about 80.53."

Now for a word or two about Ceci's game before I met her. She never had any formal instruction and played by the seat of her pants with pretty good results. Ceci is a lucky player. No matter what she does she somehow manages to land on her feet while her opponents and her partner look at one another in amazement.

Now that I have entered into the picture and tried to discipline her game a bit, one can understand the trying times we are going through.

*For the record, I met Ceci (and Minny) a few years after Phyllis could no longer put up with my bidding.

The hardest thing for me to do is to try to explain to Ceci after one of her incredible bids has just given us another top that, perhaps, it wasn't the best of all possible actions.

For example, her conception of the penalty double has either advanced or set *my* game back some 20 odd years.

To give you an idea, Ceci believes the best penalty doubles are made when you have a fit in your partner's suit and not too many of the opponent's trumps. This idea seemed rather wild to me at first, but as time went by, I began to see the infinite wisdom it contained.

Both sides vul.
Dealer West

                            North
                            ♠ 10 7 6
                            ♡ 10 9 8
                            ◇ J 9 8 5
                            ♣ 10 8 2

West (Ceci)   **East**
♠ A K 9 2   ♠ J 4 3
♡ A K Q   ♡ J 7 6 5 2
◇ Q 10 7 6 3   ◇ A 4
♣ J   ♣ A 9 5

                            South
                            ♠ Q 8 5
                            ♡ 4 3
                            ◇ K 2
                            ♣ K Q 7 6 4 3

The bidding:

West	North	East	South
1◇	Pass	1♡	2♣
Double!	Pass	Pass	Pass

Opening lead: K♡

Strangely enough when most experts were given Ceci's hand as a rebid problem, not one found the "obvious" double. After three rounds of hearts declarer could come up with no more than five trump tricks and went down 800 peacefully.

Tactfully I mentioned to Ceci that perhaps her trump holding left a little to be desired for such a low level penalty double. She nodded. Only a few days later did I understand the full significance of that nod.

Both sides vul.
Dealer East

```
                        North
                        ♠ 10 8 6
                        ♡ 8 7 6 3
                        ◇ 9 2
                        ♣ K J 9 3

West                                          East
♠ K 9 4 2                                     ♠ Q 7 5
♡ None                                        ♡ A J
◇ K J 7 6 3                                   ◇ A Q 8 4
♣ A 8 4 2                                     ♣ Q 10 7 5

                        South
                        ♠ A J 3
                        ♡ K Q 10 9 5 4 2
                        ◇ 10 5
                        ♣ 6
```

The bidding:

East	South	West	North
1 NT	3 ♡	Double!	Pass
Pass	Pass		

Opening lead: 2 ♠

Guess who doubled? Of course, the hand was defeated one trick and we have no game, so all explanation was futile. However, now

that I think of it, Ceci and I have a private understanding which
we do not put on our convention cards. When Ceci doubles for
penalties she denies trump length. When she does have their suit,
she bids notrump. Ah well, no wonder I wasn't winning anything
until I met her.

To further compound this madness, Ceci tried it my way twice
and doubled for penalties when she had four and five trumps.
They made it both times, and as inevitable as death and taxes
came "you see what happens when you have too many trumps,
they get in your way."

To try to stop Ceci from underleading aces against suit contracts is equally fruitless.

Both sides vul.
Dealer North

```
                        North
                        ♠ 7 6 5 4
                        ♡ K J 8
                        ◇ K 4
                        ♣ K 7 6 5

      West (Ceci)                              East
      ♠ 10                                     ♠ A 9 8
      ♡ A 9 7 5 2                              ♡ Q 10 6 4 3
      ◇ 9 8 5 2                                ◇ A 3
      ♣ Q 10 4                                 ♣ 9 8 2

                        South
                        ♠ K Q J 3 2
                        ♡ None
                        ◇ Q J 10 7 6
                        ♣ A J 3
```

The bidding:

North	East	South	West
Pass	Pass	1♠	Pass
3♠	Pass	4♠	All Pass

Opening lead: 5 ♡

After all, what else would one lead on this bidding? Declarer woodenly played the jack and ruffed my queen. The king of spades was taken by the ace and a heart returned. If declarer ruffs, he must later lose either a heart or a trump trick (by being forced to ruff a third heart with an honor) so he discarded. We were the only pair in the room to hold declarer to four.

Not having had enough success by underleading five to the ace, Ceci was now playing against the same declarer a few days later.

East-West vul.
Dealer East

                              North
                              ♠ 10 8 4 2
                              ♡ A J 10 5
                              ◇ A J 5
                              ♣ K Q

West (Ceci)   **East**
♠ K   ♠ A J 9 5
♡ 9 8 6   ♡ K Q 3
◇ 10 9 7   ◇ 6 2
♣ A 10 8 6 4 3   ♣ J 9 7 5

                              South
                              ♠ Q 7 6 3
                              ♡ 7 4 2
                              ◇ K Q 8 4 3
                              ♣ 2

The bidding:

East	South	West	North
Pass	Pass	Pass	1◇
Double	1♠	Pass!	2♣
Pass	Pass	Pass	

When I asked Ceci later why she didn't mention her clubs, she said that if she bid them and everyone passed, she would have to play the hand. For a moment I had completely forgotten how Ceci's mind works.

Anyway if you don't bid a six-card suit headed by the ace-ten, you surely lead it—I mean you surely underlead it! The opening lead was the six of clubs! Notice the honesty. Always fourth best.

Too bad the KJ doubleton wasn't in dummy, but declarer won the first trick and led a trump. I played low and declarer, placing me with the ace-king of spades, played the queen. Ceci won the king and hopefully laid down the ace of clubs which declarer ruffed. I said nothing nor did I look at Ceci. (You will learn why later.)

Slightly bewildered by this turn of events, declarer led another trump. I then drew all of the remaining trumps and we ran our club suit to defeat the hand three tricks.

After the hand, declarer, who was still fuming, asked Ceci if she always underled aces. "Only when I have them," was the reply.

One of the main reasons my position in Ceci's affections is a losing fourth is that my behavior at the bridge table is not always optimum. For example, if I violate any of the following rules (commandments), there is no telling how far downward I might spiral.

RULES FOR EDWIN TO REMEMBER
WHEN PLAYING WITH CECI

1. Always, but always, look at any dummy Ceci puts down with love and affection—no matter how hideous it might really be.

2. Never, never say a cross word or give anything but adoring looks across the table no matter how much the urge to "kill" surges from within.

3. Never concede the rest of the tricks to the opponents even though declarer has seven cards remaining—six high trumps and an ace—and Ceci has a small trump. Somehow declarer might forget about Ceci's deuce and she might be able to trump that ace.

4. No matter how many suits Ceci bids, it does not necessarily mean she has those suits, she just wants me to bid notrump . . . "For God's sake, I thought you never were going to bid it."

5. Get the best possible teammates for any local event even if it means making a long distance call to Rome for Garozzo and Belladonna.

6. Win!

We have yet to cover Ceci's play of the hand or her slam bidding. Here is an example of what goes on in my mind when I watch Ceci play a hand.

North-South vul.
Dealer North

North (me)
♠ None
♡ A K 9 3
♢ J 7 6 3 2
♣ Q J 10 7

The bidding:

North	East	South	West
Pass	1♠	Pass	2♠
Double	Pass	2 NT	Pass
3 ♢	3♠	3 NT	All Pass

Another logical auction with Ceci. I couldn't stand two notrump so, naturally, Ceci bid three notrump. And of course she doesn't double three spades so I know she must be loaded in that suit.

Anyway a spade is led and I figure that Ceci must have a big diamond fit with me (if I were playing with Marshall Miles, I would bet that he had at least five diamonds) and is counting on running that suit.

Ceci's first discard from the dummy is a diamond. Wrong again! The next card out of her hand is the queen of diamonds! First she discards one, then she plays one . . . Dear God, I must be going crazy! I must stop worrying about what she is doing because it almost always works out. The whole deal:

```
                        North
                        ♠ None
                        ♡ A K 9 3
                        ◇ J 7 6 3 2
                        ♣ Q J 10 7
West                                        East
♠ J 6 2                                     ♠ Q 8 7 5 4 3
♡ 10 4                                      ♡ Q J 8 7
◇ K 5                                       ◇ A 9 4
♣ K 9 8 6 3 2                               ♣ None
                        South
                        ♠ A K 10 9
                        ♡ 6 5 2
                        ◇ Q 10 8
                        ♣ A 5 4
```

When the smoke cleared, Ceci had made four notrump and was beaming; (the jack of spades was led—we were playing in a tough field) and doubling three spades would hardly have been worthwhile as declarer can get out for down one.

Without giving you a full description of another hand Ceci played, I must tell you about her management of a suit combination.

```
                        North (me)
                        ◇ A K Q 4 3
West                                        East
◇ 9 5                                       ◇ J 8 6 2
                        South (Ceci)
                        ◇ 10 7
```

Ceci was playing a heart partial and diamonds was dummy's first bid suit. West led the nine of diamonds. My attention wandered for a moment, and later as I looked down at the trick, I saw that Ceci had called a low diamond from dummy and had won the trick with the ten!

Now I was angry at myself for not steering the hand to my beloved notrump as Ceci apparently had the jack and ten of diamonds even though I had mentioned (sweetly) that she should win these tricks with the higher of equal cards.

As Ceci pondered the dummy (a rarity), I glanced into my left hand opponent's hand (soon to be another no-no) and lo and behold there was the jack of diamonds!

Mixed emotions set in. At least Ceci had not forgotten about taking tricks with the higher of equals but how in blazes did she make her ten of diamonds, why did she duck, and how come East (a competent player) still had the jack of diamonds?

It developed that Ceci meant to call for a high diamond but she said small instead. East was so sure she was going to call for a high diamond that he also ducked and at least that mystery was solved.

I hate to add this, but later in the hand Ceci played off two high diamonds and West ruffed. West in turn put her partner back in to play the jack of diamonds, and although I'm not sure, I think Ceci finally wound up losing an extra trick by ducking the *!%†!% diamond lead in the first place.

Ceci is not beneath taking an occasional practice finesse if the situation demands it. The definition of a practice finesse is, in case you are interested, a finesse which, if it works, gives you the same number of tricks you would have taken if you had not finessed at all. But it does keep you in practice.

[Witness this hand: see top of next column]

East-West vul.
Dealer North

                              North
                              ♠ J 10 6 5
                              ♡ K J 10 9 8 7
                              ◇ 5
                              ♣ Q 7

West   East
♠ 7 3   ♠ A 8
♡ Q 6 5   ♡ 3 2
◇ K 10 8 7   ◇ A J 4 3
♣ A 10 6 2   ♣ K 9 8 5 4

                              South (Ceci)
                              ♠ K Q 9 4 2
                              ♡ A 4
                              ◇ Q 9 6 2
                              ♣ J 3

The bidding:

North	East	South	West
Pass	Pass	1♠	Pass
3♠	Pass	Pass	Pass

Opening lead: 3 ♣

East won the trick and returned a club to West's ace. West, a clever soul, played another trump, thus giving Ceci a chance to do a little "practicing."

Notice that if Ceci plays the ace-king and a third heart, ruffing, she can then get back to dummy with a trump, discard a club and two diamonds on the hearts and concede a diamond to make four.

However, the more aesthetic way to make four is to play the ace and finesse the jack of hearts! Now if the finesse loses, you are down one, but if it works you get rid of one club and three diamonds and still make four.

Ceci took the finesse ("West could have had four hearts, Edwin *darling*"). Naturally it worked, and naturally we got a good result. Most of the pairs were in four going down one which Ceci was quick to point out to me as she gazed at the other scores on the pickup slip.

Ceci has recently given me another rule which states in no uncertain terms that we must bid any slam that makes.

This, in turn, puts a little (just a little, mind you) pressure on me who, even without these ultimatums, has a tough enough time on slam hands.

It turns out Ceci and I missed a good seven hearts on these two hands which cost us a Swiss Team match.

Opener (Ceci)	Responder (Me)
♠ 4 2	♠ A Q 10 9 5
♡ A K 8 7 4 3	♡ Q 6
◇ A K Q 6 5	◇ J 10
♣ None	♣ A Q 9 4

Opener	Responder
1 ♡	1 ♠
3 ◇	3 ♡
4 ♡	4 NT
5 ♡	5 NT
6 ♡	6 NT
Pass	

With the hearts breaking 3-2, there was no problem in the play. (It seemed to me that once Ceci knew that I had both black aces — when I bid 5 NT, I promised all four aces held jointly — she might have bid the grand slam taking the slight gamble that I had the queen of hearts.)

We had missed a grand slam and that was not so good. Then this one came up shortly thereafter:

North (dealer)
♠ Q 5 4 3
♡ A Q 10 6 5 4
◇ 5 4
♣ 3

South
♠ None
♡ J 9 2
◇ A K 7 3
♣ A K Q 8 4 2

The bidding:
(Ceci)

North	East	South	West
Pass	Pass	1 ♣	Pass
1 ♡	1 ♠	2 ◇	Pass
2 ♡	Pass	2 ♠	Pass
3 ♣ !	Pass	5 ♡	All Pass

Lead: K ♠

Making seven with the heart finesse onside. Well, this called for a little discussion. It turned out that my spade cue bid had confused her and her spade raise had scared her. That is why we did not reach this slam although we did agree that my jump to five was asking about the quality of her trump suit.

So that was two slams down the tubes and even Minny (the maltese, remember?) was getting restless watching this ineptness. Then came this number:

North-South vul.
Dealer East

                          North (Ceci)
                          ♠ A
                          ♡ 7 6
                          ◇ 10 5 4
                          ♣ A 10 9 6 5 3 2

West   **East**
♠ K J 9 5 4 3 2   ♠ 10 7 6
♡ 8   ♡ A J 10 5 4 3
◇ 7 6 3   ◇ J 8 2
♣ J 4   ♣ Q

                          South (me)
                          ♠ Q 8
                          ♡ K Q 9 2
                          ◇ A K Q 9
                          ♣ K 8 7

East	South	West	North
2♡ (Weak)	3 NT		

At this point West asked Ceci what my 3 NT bid meant. Ceci answered that it was forcing to game. West passed and Ceci leaped to six no trump, the only slam that makes. A heart ruff will beat any suit slam.

But our very best hand was the following:

East-West vul.
Dealer North

North (me)
♠ A K Q 7 6
♡ None
◇ 6 5 3
♣ Q 8 7 6 4

South (Ceci)
♠ 5 3
♡ 7 6 3
◇ K J 4
♣ A K J 9 3

North	East	South	West
1 ♠*	Pass	2 ♣	Pass
3 ♣	Pass	3 ◇	Pass
3 ♡	Double	4 ♣	Pass
6 ♣	Pass	Pass	Pass

*In my book I recommend opening these minimum 5-5 black hands with one club — but that book was written before I met Ceci and she has altered my bidding style somewhat.

At this point West asked Ceci about the meaning of my three-heart bid. Ceci's answer would have gladdened the heart of any partner. "Oh, he's either asking me or telling me something, I don't know, and I don't care."

A heart was led, Ceci ruffed, drew trumps in two rounds, and set up the spades (they were 4-2) for two diamond discards to make a slam with only 23 high card points between the combined hands.

Who knows, maybe I will get to third place one of these days.

Tales Out of School

**A Teacher Tells of the Wild and Wacky Things
That They Can't Teach You in Bridge Class**

It has been estimated that there are in the vicinity of 70,000,000 bridge players in the United States.

To the novice player that figure seems somewhat high but reasonable. The average player doesn't really believe it; the expert player knows in his heart that there are no more than 10 bridge players in all the land while the bridge teacher wonders if there is even one.

The teacher of beginning and intermediate bridge classes is doomed to a life of frustration. Most of his students simply will not play between lessons and those who do are subjected to so much advice from their friends who are "expert" players that they seldom, if ever, can recover from this compendium of misinformation.

Let's start with a few of my own experiences from beginning classes which I no longer teach. The reason I no longer teach beginners is that I was afraid I would forget how to play myself if I continued. Their logic is so illogical that sooner or later I begin to fall victim to it. To wit:

In all my classes I have the students distribute the cards. Each one starts with an entire suit and I instruct them, one suit at a time, how to divide the cards.

After five lessons of this type of distribution one lady who had yet to distribute the diamonds suddenly thought she had been dealt thirteen of them! In the middle of the class she jumped up and screamed, "Alice, you wouldn't believe this hand!"

Then there was the lady who went wild over singletons. On one hand she was dealt only twelve cards including a singleton spade. She called me over to help her straighten out the hand. I found the missing card on the floor, it was the ace of spades. As I placed it in her hand she told me, "Now you've gone and wrecked my hand."

I have learned, after many bitter years, that most players simply do not know their directions. Nowadays I place directional guide cards on the table and point North at the blackboard. I do this because I chalk the hand that they are playing and it becomes somewhat easier for them to orient themselves. What I mean is, it should be easier. I have one group in Pasadena who simply will not play unless North is placed the same way that it is in Pasadena.

Then this happened to me. I occasionally teach private lessons at home. This particular group of four ladies was very eager to brush up on their game because they hadn't played for a long time.

So I went to one of their homes and as each of the "girls" came in, there was much to be said about beauty parlors, dresses, divorces, marriages, etc.

On the very first hand one lady after sorting her cards started placing some threes face up on the table. I asked her what she was doing. "Oh, she replied, I thought we were playing canasta."

A few months later in yet another beginning class I found out how cruel a person I really was.

Declarer was playing the hand in spades. In dummy was the A J 5 of diamonds and in her own hand the singleton deuce. The opening lead was the king of diamonds which declarer captured with the ace. Later in the hand the opening leader tried to cash the queen of diamonds which declarer ruffed. As I left the table for a few seconds I saw that declarer was correctly drawing trumps.

Upon returning I found that everyone was discussing something or other. I casually asked declarer if the jack of diamonds in the dummy was a good trick or not. She looked up at me and said, "we were just talking over spades, and now you ask about diamonds. What are you, a sadist or something?"

For some reason whenever I give an illustration of how a particular suit should be played, I make the suit spades. In this case I was showing when the queen should be played from the queen-jack. (Usually when partner leads the king.) After the class is over one fellow comes up to me and asks me to settle a bet. His wife is betting him that the only suit you can drop the queen from the queen-jack is in spades. Beautiful.

Then there was the lady who was playing a notrump contract with the A K Q 2 of hearts on the table and the J 4 3 in her own hand. At one point she had to make a discard from the table and she wanted to discard the deuce of hearts even though she needed four tricks from that suit to make her contract.

As she was reaching for the deuce of hearts, a slightly over emotional "no" came from me. This naturally caused her to drop all of her cards face up on the table. After we retrieved them, I pointed out by placing the jack on the deuce that by careful play this suit could actually be brought in for four tricks.

She shook her head disgustedly. "I missed that key play, didn't I?" As I was leaving the table I heard one opponent say to the other — "do you think we'll ever be able to see things like that?"

Then there is a certain group who tell themselves, no matter how many mistakes they make, that they are coming to class just to pass time, and that they really know everything that I'm telling them. The reasons that I have heard for their mistakes are:

1. I can't play when he is watching.

2. They're all trick hands anyway.

3. I wouldn't bid, play, defend, (choose any three) that way if it wasn't a lesson.

4. Too much pressure around here.

5. I have better partners when I play at home.

6. We're just not trying.

7. Oh, he thinks he's so smart with those key plays of his.

Then there are the superstitious ones. "I never bid slams, they never make." "I don't like hands with four aces." "I never finesse with eight cards missing the queen, I don't care what the rule says." Also from the same lady, "the player who holds the nine always has the queen, I don't care."

Once I was called to fill in for a hand. I was the dealer and these were the two hands:

Opener (me)	Responder (she)
♠ 10 4	♠ A K J 5
♡ A Q 9 7 6	♡ J 10 3
◇ Q 10 4	◇ A K
♣ A 7 6	♣ K 10 8 5

Our advanced bidding went like this:

Me	She
1♡	4 NT
5♡	6♡
Pass	

Me to she: "Why did you jump to 4 NT so quickly, I might have had a four card heart suit."

She to me: What do you mean, four? You rebid them, didn't you?

Then there was the advanced, advanced lesson on endplays. As I came over to one table I asked the declarer, a particularly pretty young thing, if she played for the endplay. "No," she replied, "I decided to play for a revoke instead."

"And how did you do that," I asked naively.

"Oh," she answered, "I switched suits at every trick."

Then there are the rabble rousers. All my classes know by now that I do not play five card majors and that I avoid opening three card club suits if possible. Merely by admitting that, I have alienated myself more than if I had admitted to being a Communist.

This one man brings up this hand written on a piece of paper: ♠AKJ10 ♡KJ10 ◇Q54 ♣J94 and asks me what I would open. Before anything, I tell him, "you know I avoid opening a short club."

He says he does too, he would much rather open with a short dia-mond!

One week I gave a lesson on the Stayman Convention and the following week I was watching a player who held: ♠A1054 ♡KQ87 ◇654 ♣65. Her right hand opponent opened 1D and she over-called, naturally, with 2 C. "What are you doing," I asked. "Oh, I was making a Stayman," she replied.

Then there was the cagey declarer. In 7 NT the last three cards around the table were:

North
♠ none
♡ none
◇ none
♣ K J 2

West
♠ none
♡ A
◇ none
♣ Q 5

East
♠ none
♡ none
◇ none
♣ 10 9 8

South
♠ none
♡ 9
◇ none
♣ A 3

Declarer had yet to lose a trick and the lead was in his own hand. Things look pretty good, right? Wrong. Declarer led a low club to the king and then a low club back to the ace, even though he knew his nine of hearts was not high, and eventually conceded a trick to the ace of that suit.

As this play was made by a very intelligent person, I couldn't resist asking him what was going through his mind.

It turned out that he originally had the queen of hearts in his hand which he had discarded for deceptive purposes, retaining the nine. In the end he confessed that he had been so impressed with his own discard that he wanted to see if he had fooled anyone.

Sometimes I am overcome with guilt feelings and I can't help but warn them about the traps I have set for them. For example, this deal:

Both sides vul.
Dealer West

                          North
                          ♠ 7 4
                          ♡ A K 5
                          ◇ A K 10 9 8 7
                          ♣ A 2

West   **East**
♠ A Q 9 3 2   ♠ 10 8 5
♡ J 10 7 6   ♡ 9 8
◇ 2   ◇ J 5 4 3
♣ K Q 10   ♣ 8 7 6 5

                          South
                          ♠ K J 6
                          ♡ Q 4 3 2
                          ◇ Q 6
                          ♣ J 9 4 3

The bidding:

West	North	East	South
1♠	Double	Pass	2♡
Pass	3◇	Pass	3 NT
Pass	Pass	Pass	

Opening lead: 3♠

The gist of the hand is for South to win the spade opening, cross to a high heart and run the ten of diamonds. This is a safety play to guard against East having four diamonds to the jack and being able to punch a spade through South's king.

From bitter experience I know that this hand is a bit much for an intermediate class, so I warned them to be careful of the diamond suit.

One lady took my warning so to heart that she won the spade opening and played the ace and a low club ducking the trick to West's queen. It was now easy for her to establish her ninth trick in clubs without monkeying with diamonds at all!

Then, of course, there are the sleepers. This I don't mind as long as they don't snore. They are invariably husbands who have been literally dragged along by their wives to learn "the finer points".

Some of the sleepers will take an occasional nap but this one fellow goes soundly to sleep the minute I open my mouth.

During the lesson on third hand play I always throw in this hand:

Both sides vul.
Dealer North

```
                    North
                    ♠ A J 4
                    ♡ 7 6
                    ◇ 8 7
                    ♣ A Q J 8 7 6

    West                            East
    ♠ 7 6 5                         ♠ 10 9 3 2
    ♡ Q 10 2                        ♡ A 5 4 3
    ◇ K 9 4 3 2                     ◇ Q J 5
    ♣ 4 3                           ♣ K 2

                    South
                    ♠ K Q 8
                    ♡ K J 9 8
                    ◇ A 10 6
                    ♣ 10 9 5
```

The bidding:

North	East	South	West
1 ♣	Pass	2 NT	Pass
3 NT	All Pass		

or

North	East	South	West
1 ♣	Pass	1 ♡	Pass
2 ♣	Pass	3 NT	All Pass

Opening lead: 3 ◇

I have learned to always put at least two bidding sequences on the board for each hand. If I don't someone will always ask if they couldn't bid the hand another way.

In any case I have explained at length before the hand is distributed that third hand should play the lower or lowest of touching honors when partner leads a small card and dummy also has small cards.

On the actual hand I simply wanted East to play the jack, then the queen, and finally a low diamond to South's ace. When South eventually finesses clubs East is supposed to lead a LOW heart trying to put West in to run the diamonds. South is supposed to go up with the king because the hand cannot be made if West has the ace of hearts, so South might as well play East for that card.

Yes, I know that this hand can be beaten if, after winning the first two diamonds, East shifts to a low heart immediately. The defense must then come to two diamonds, two hearts and a club. However, this defense has never been found until . . . until my sleeper picked up the East cards. This was his defense, never having heard a word of the lesson, naturally.

At trick one he played the queen of diamonds, of course. When South ducked he returned a LOW HEART. Now South finessed the jack and West won the queen and played a low diamond! The fact that South must have the ace and jack never bothered her. When East put up the jack, South was forced to duck again. My sleeper continued with another low heart and when declarer finessed the nine West won the ten and the hand was defeated two tricks while at most other tables the hand was being made. What should I say? And what difference would it make. He was already sleeping.

Then, of course, we deal with the most common type of all. The nervous player. She is afraid that every time she breathes she is making a mistake, and if her partner sneezes, she is a ten to one shot to drop her cards. The nervous player tends to become very emotional if, for example, something exciting like a finesse works.

Recently this combination of cards arose in a lesson hand:

	North	
	◇ A 4 3 2	
West		East
◇ K 8 7		◇ 10 6 5
	South	
	◇ Q J 9	

This was the lesson on second hand play and the idea was for West not to cover the queen of diamonds from the closed hand because it might expose East to a finesse if declarer had Q J 9. I might add at this point, in 15 years of teaching only three West players have not covered the queen, so indoctrinated are they to cover an honor with an honor.

Anyway, at this table the queen was covered, naturally, and declarer in a moment of monumental inspiration won the ace, finessed the nine on the way back, cashed the jack and set up the four of diamonds for the contract-making discard. Feeling safe that declarer would use the four of diamonds to discard her obvious loser I made my usual error of leaving the table prematurely. Upon returning I saw the four of diamonds on the table and the opponents taking the setting trick because declarer had neglected to use the card.

I finally asked her what she did with her last diamond. She then pointed to it and said, "it's right there, I was too excited to do anything with it."

Then there is one table of women that I will never forget. I know secretly why they come to my classes . . . to torment each other. They have no greater pleasure than to see a mistake being made, even if by their own partner.

It would all be fairly humorous if they would only keep quiet once in a while. There is no way I can get a word in edgewise to the class until they are through chewing each other out. Rather than get angry I decided to listen to what they were saying to one another. This is the way it usually went:

"Let me alone, I didn't lead the deuce, you did." "I did not, I didn't even have the deuce. You know what he says about deuces anyway." "I don't care what he says about deuces, you led one, so let me alone." "Shh he's going to explain, let's listen and see who had the deuce and you let me alone."

Among the most dangerous of all students are the "rule memorizers" and the "convention experts."

My "rule experts" always lead trumps because they are "forever in doubt." They never lead away from a king because it is a gigantic no-no. They lead through strength even if that strength consists of A K Q J x and they still lead the highest card in their partner's suit because their great grandmother did. Those, of course, are the old-fashioned "rule experts". The modern variety offer something new and dashing to the scene.

In one lesson I was trying to help them read the opponents' leads. I mentioned that if a deuce was led, particularly at no-trump, the opening leader would have a four card suit and it would therefore be simple to know how many cards his partner held.

I made a particular point of mentioning the value of the small cards because if the opening leader is leading his smallest card he usually has a four card suit. Therefore, if the four is led and the three and deuce are visible the opening leader has four cards, whereas if either the three or the deuce is invisible the opening leader can have a five card suit if he has the missing card.

From the back of the room. "Does this mean the rule of eleven doesn't work anymore?"

Now for a word from our conventions expert. Once again I was explaining when an honor should be covered and when it shouldn't. (I am so convincing when I give this lecture that I almost forget how many mistakes I have made in this same situation.)

We were going over the typical situation where the student is West:

North (Dummy)
♠ A 4 3

West
♠ K 7 6

South
♠ Q

I mentioned that if a decent South player leads the queen the presumption is that the closed hand contains the jack as well. And, if we could *see* both the queen and the jack, we would cover the second honor; so should we wait for the jack to be led. "But what if they are playing Rusinow leads?"*

Nor can we overlook a species known the world over: "the mad signaller," and his country cousin "the impossible or random discarder". It is literally 1000-to-1 that if one of these players makes either a signal or a discard it will cost an average of 1.563 tricks per deal.

In order to help out these poor misguided souls I have given them a few rules to follow, especially if I ever play with them professionally.

I have in mind one fellow in particular whose signalling and discarding were what you might term mildly "far out".

I told him that I would prefer he didn't signal me at all as I usually could tell what was going on anyway. (The translation of this is — after the hand is over I always know what I should have done.)

*Rusinow leads refers to a special convention used by the DEFENDERS on opening lead wherein the lower of two touching honors is led first.

And as for discarding:

1. Always keep the same length as dummy.
2. Do not discard down to a void.
3. Do not discard from a suit declarer has bid, or at least try and keep the same number of cards that you think declarer has in the suit.
4. As a general rule, discard from a suit you do not want led so you can preserve length and strength in the suit or suits you do want led.

With this as background you can imagine the torment that must have been going on in his mind during the defense of the following hand:

Neither side vul.
Dealer North

                        North
                        ♠ K J 10 9 8
                        ♡ A K 8 3
                        ◇ 7 6
                        ♣ 8 5

West   East (teacher)
♠ Q 7 6 5 4   ♠ A 3 2
♡ 10   ♡ Q 9 7 5 2
◇ Q 8 5 4 3 2   ◇ J 9
♣ 7   ♣ K 6 3

                        South
                        ♠ None
                        ♡ J 6 4
                        ◇ A K 10
                        ♣ A Q J 10 9 4 2

Playing against weak opponents the bidding went:

North	East	South	West
1 ♠	Pass	2 ♣	Pass
2 ♡	Pass	3 ◇	Pass
3 ♠	Pass	3 NT	All Pass

My boy decided to lead the ten of hearts which was ducked to my queen. Having a perfect picture of the whole hand I decided to return a heart to kill dummy's entry to the spade suit. (On target, as usual.) Anyway I led back a heart and when declarer played the jack I think I actually saw perspiration on my partner's forehead. You see he had to make a discard, and every discard would violate a rule! A spade was out because he had the same length as dummy; a diamond was out because declarer had bid that suit and he had to keep as many as declarer! A club was out because he was not supposed to void himself in any suit.

After much soul-searching he finally discarded the seven of clubs. Declarer, who was taken to believe everything at face value, decided my partner had the king of clubs and it was fruitless to take the finesse. After all a seven is a seven is a seven.

Finally declarer played the ace and queen of clubs to my king. Don't ask what torture my partner underwent during these two plays. I finally cashed my ace of spades to hold the hand to four notrump for a clear top.

My other good board playing professionally still sticks with me.

North
♠ K 4
♡ K 10 2
◇ K 10 9 8 7
♣ 7 6 5

West (me)
♠ 9 8 7 6 5
♡ 3
◇ J 6 5
♣ A 4 3 2

East (she)
♠ A Q 3 2
♡ Q 4
◇ 4 3
♣ K J 10 9 8

South
♠ J 10
♡ A J 9 8 7 6 5
◇ A Q 2
♣ Q

Our bidding:

West	North	East	South
Pass	Pass	3♣!	4♡
Pass	Pass	Pass	

Opening lead: A♣

Although it is true that we can make four spades nobody was in it and four hearts was making at every table . . . except ours. We beat it!

After scoring my ace of clubs I shifted to a spade at trick two. My partner scored two spade tricks and returned the king of clubs. Declarer fearing a singleton club in my hand ruffed with the ace of hearts and my partner's queen of trump became the setting trick.

Bridge is a lovely game, I love to teach, and in my other world of expert players I don't have nearly as much fun.

Wot's Da Bid?

Challenge. Someone had a brilliancy. Why not pit four famous athletes, all reasonably good bridge players, against the two-time World Champion U.S. Aces in a six deal board-a-match exhibition?

But what chance would the athletes have in such a match? Actually they would have two chances. Slim and none. So what could be done to equalize the match? Now for the real brilliancy. The athletes would be allowed to LOOK AT EACH OTHER'S HANDS FOR FIFTEEN SECONDS BEFORE BEGINNING THE BIDDING AND AN ADDITIONAL FIVE SECOND EXCHANGE WOULD BE MADE IF THEY WERE ON OPENING LEAD.

Now, who do you like in this match scheduled at the Lancaster, Pa. Fall Nationals? In addition I was asked to prepare the hands and to double as coach of the athletes. *Now* who do you like in this match?

Choice. Who was my team? Well for starters I had Jim Bunning, the only ball player in history to pitch no hitters in both the American and National Leagues. But could he pitch curves at the Aces? Then there was Tim McCarver, catcher, and a World Series hero when he played with the St. Louis Cardinals. But could he throw out any of the Aces when they tried stealing? It was obvious that these two should play together. For my other pair I had Richie Ashburn, two-time National League Batting champion and for the past ten years a baseball announcer for his beloved Phillies. Ashburn, in his day, was one of the fastest men in baseball. But could he move fast enough to steal any tricks from the Aces? For his partner we tried another sport, golf. We had Frank Beard, one of the very best in the world, but could he chip anything past those Aces? Time would tell.

Champs. The Aces were at the time down to four players. They went with Bobby Wolff, ping pong champion of his block, and Bob Hamman who looks mean enough to be a great blocking back but in fact has trouble tackling his son Chris, age five. At the other table were those two tennis champions Bobby Goldman and Mike Lawrence. Both showed other skills as well in Lancaster. Lawrence was the number one pin ball machine expert in the place with no exception. Goldman also retained his position in Lancaster as No. 1 girlwatcher with no exceptions, although Don Krauss and I are always in there pitching.

Strategy. Our team decided to have a pre-match dinner to discuss strategy. It was my opinion that since the players would be able to see each other's hands it might be (1) wise to bid to what we think we can make in one bid without letting those nasty Aces in on our distribution and (2) if we see that the hand belongs to them maybe we should bid one of their best suits. *Now* who do you like in this match?

Everyone on my squad thought that both were super ideas, particularly Beard and McCarver who couldn't wait to do the Aces in. Ashburn, who must have been the cockiest of ball players, couldn't understand how the Aces could possibly win and already was asking where the next big tournament was when I reminded him that at the next tournament he wouldn't be allowed to look at his partner's hand.

Now for the match!

East-West vul.
Dealer South

North
♠ K 9 5
♡ 2
◇ A 9 6 5
♣ 7 6 4 3 2

West   **East**
♠ J 8 4   ♠ Q 10 3 2
♡ 10 9   ♡ 8 7 6
◇ Q 10 8 7 4 3   ◇ 2
♣ K Q   ♣ J 10 9 8 5

South
♠ A 7 6
♡ A K Q J 5 4 3
◇ K J
♣ A

The bidding in the Closed Room was fast and furious:

South	West	North	East
Beard	**Goldman**	**Ashburn**	**Lawrence**
6 ♡	Pass	Pass	Pass

Blunder. Beard took his twelve obvious tricks to score 980 for the ballplayers. This was a board I expected the Aces to win because 13 tricks can be made at hearts via a double squeeze and Hamman makes double squeezes in his sleep even if he does have trouble tackling Christopher. (Can you see how?)

Now for the bidding in the Open Room, the Vu Graph room.

South	West	North	East
Hamman	McCarver	Wolff	Bunning
1♣*	4♣!**	Double	Pass
4♡	5♢!!***	Double	Pass
Pass	Pass		

*Seventeen or more high card points.

**Oh, my God.

***I knew I shouldn't have mentioned anything in our pre-game warm up. And vulnerable!

When the smoke cleared, and it took a while, McCarver was the proud possessor of three tricks, down eight for a slight loss of 2300 points. *Now* who do you like in this match?

By the way, thirteen tricks can be made at hearts by winning the lead, drawing trumps, playing two high diamonds ending in dummy and ruffing a club. Now the remaining trumps are played leaving this position with one trump to be played:

North
♠ K 9
♡ none
♢ 9
♣ 7

West
♠ J 8 4
♡ none
♢ 10
♣ none

East
♠ Q 10 3
♡ none
♢ none
♣ J

South
♠ A 7 6
♡ 4
♢ none
♣ none

On the last trump West is obliged to discard a spade, dummy a diamond and East is caught in a black suit squeeze.

Regroup. Board II had a little bit for everyone. (Players and seats have been rearranged so that South is the declarer.)

East-West vul.
Dealer East

```
                        North
                        ♠ K 9 2
                        ♡ A 10 5 4
                        ◇ K Q
                        ♣ A 7 3 2

        West                                    East
        ♠ Q 7 6                                 ♠ 10 5
        ♡ None                                  ♡ J 9 8 7 6 3
        ◇ 9 8 4 3 2                             ◇ 7 5
        ♣ K Q J 9 4                             ♣ 10 8 5

                        South
                        ♠ A J 8 4 3
                        ♡ K Q 2
                        ◇ A J 10 6
                        ♣ 6
```

This was my most diabolical deal—designed to make whichever Ace was sitting South hate me forever. You see, I thought that the Aces would bid to six spades, a beautiful contract, and the declarer would surely make a safety play in spades—ace and low to the nine. This would result in East making his doubleton ten and then giving West a heart ruff.

In the Open Room the bidding followed expected lines. Hamman, East, passed and McCarver, naturally, opened the bidding six spades. What else? He won the Club lead and, disdaining the safety play, simply played the king of spades and then low to the jack. Wolff won the queen but that was the Aces' last trick. + 980 to the athletes.

The real action took place in the Closed Room. This was the bidding.

East	South	West	North
Beard	Goldman	Ashburn	Lawrence
Pass	1 ♠	Pass	2 ♣
Pass	2 ◇	Pass	2 ♠*
Pass	2 NT	Pass	3 ♡
Pass	3 NT	Pass	Pass
Double!	Pass	Pass	4 ♠
Pass	Pass	Pass	

*Forcing to game

Fear. Well the Aces had their chance to win the board. They had to redouble three no trump and divine the spade position. But as it was Lawrence was afraid of the club lead and a possible spade loser. After all, his opponents had doubled three notrump after they had exchanged hands! It is enough to unnerve a man, you know.

Anyway Goldman made six spades but he wasn't in it so that evened the match at one-all.

Actually it was becoming pretty difficult to predict who was going to win this match. Let it be recorded that at this point Ashburn suggested that the athletes also be allowed to look at the Aces hands before the bidding started but that was quickly vetoed.

Error. Board III brought the Vu Graph crowd, already in a hysterical state, to their feet when Hamman-Wolff had a misunderstanding that they have been trying to explain away ever since.

East-West vul.
Dealer South

                        North
                        ♠ J 10 6 2
                        ♡ A K 2
                        ◊ 10 4
                        ♣ A Q 5 3

West   East
♠ 9 7 3   ♠ 4
♡ J 9 8 7 6 4   ♡ 10 5
◊ A Q 8 5   ◊ K J 9 3 2
♣ None   ♣ J 10 9 7 6

                        South
                        ♠ A K Q 8 5
                        ♡ Q 3
                        ◊ 7 6
                        ♣ K 8 4 2

The idea, I naively imagined, was for South to play four spades
and surely make it unless West leads a low diamond, ruffs the
club return, and leads another low diamond for a second club ruff.
I didn't think the Aces would be up to that defense but perhaps
the athletes might work it out.

Misunderstanding. Well, I was partly right. In the Closed Room
Ashburn opened four spades and made five with a heart lead. This
is what happened in the Open Room—in full view of everyone.

South	West	North	East
Wolff	Bunning	Hamman	McCarver
1♠	Pass	4♣*	4◊
Pass	Pass	4♡	5◊
Pass	Pass	6♣	Pass
7♣	Pass	Pass	Pass

*Hamman thought it was Control Swiss showing five controls (ace = 2, king = 1). Wolff thought it showed a strong hand with a singleton or void plus spade support.

Anticipate. As the bidding progressed Wolff kept thinking Hamman's hand was bigger and bigger and Hamman kept thinking that Wolff must be shorter and shorter in diamonds from his failure to double that suit at the existing vulnerability. Finally they decided that the trap I had set was for them to bid seven spades on their 5-4 fit when all along they could make seven clubs on their 4-4! (By this time they were trying to outguess me and gave me credit for arranging things I had never even dreamed of.)

Seven clubs was not exactly a success story and I was told that McCarver couldn't stop laughing throughout the entire hand.

So after three boards the athletes were leading 2-1 and needing only one more win to insure at least a tie which meant a tiebreaker deal which was prepared and favored the Aces. Now for the last time, who do you like in this match?

Vu Graph. The Aces were going to have to play with mirrors to win Board IV. The result, for once, was predictable.

Neither side vul.
Dealer South

<pre>
                          North
                          ♠ A Q 5
                          ♡ 10 7 6
                          ◇ Q J 7 2
                          ♣ K J 10
     West   East
     ♠ J 10 8 4 3   ♠ 6 2
     ♡ K   ♡ A Q J 9 8
     ◇ 10 8 5   ◇ 9 6 3
     ♣ 9 6 4 2   ♣ 8 7 5
                          South
                          ♠ K 9 7
                          ♡ 5 4 3 2
                          ◇ A K 4
                          ♣ A Q 3
</pre>

The players had changed rooms so Lawrence, Goldman, Beard and Ashburn were now on Vu Graph.

In the Closed Room, Bunning, South, pitching carefully as usual, opened one club. Hamman, West, passed and McCarver wasted no time, leaping to three notrump which closed the auction. Wolff tried a heart lead, but, alas, the wrong one. He led the queen. Hamman won and shifted to a spade, McCarver taking the next ten tricks. + 430 to the athletes.

In the Open Room there was more action. The bidding went:

South	West	North	East
Lawrence	Beard	Goldman	Ashburn
1 NT	Pass	3 NT	Double
Pass	Pass	Pass	

Lead. Not content with getting a heart lead, Ashburn doubled Lawrence in three notrump. Still stinging from his previous run-out of three no doubled, Lawrence stood his ground. "Miraculously" Beard found the opening lead of the singleton king of hearts. Ashburn overtook and ran the first five heart tricks to pick up 100 points for the athletes and give them a near-commanding 3-1 lead with only two boards to go.

Surprise. Board V gave the Aces new life and although it was a board they figured to win anyway, they won it in a most peculiar manner.

North-South vul.
Dealer West

```
                    North
                    ♠ J 7
                    ♡ K J 10 3
                    ◇ 8 6
                    ♣ Q J 8 7 6
    West                              East
    ♠ A 4                            ♠ 6 2
    ♡ 9 7 6 2                        ♡ A Q 8 5 4
    ◇ A K Q 10                       ◇ J 7 4 3
    ♣ 10 4 2                         ♣ 9 5
                    South
                    ♠ K Q 10 9 8 5 3
                    ♡ None
                    ◇ 9 5 2
                    ♣ A K 3
```

My idea here was to give the Aces a chance to show off their defensive prowess. Naively, again, I figured that both South players would declare four spades against a high diamond lead.

The only defense at trick two is to shift to a low spade. Now there is no way for declarer to avoid the loss of three diamonds and a spade trick against best defense.

Shift. I could see all of the Aces making this play but I couldn't exactly picture any of my own players finding this shift. (Heresy.) But this is what actually happened:

Closed Room:

West	North	East	South
Bunning	Hamman	McCarver	Wolff
1◇	Pass	4♡	4♠
Double	Pass	Pass	Pass

Opening lead: K◇

As I heard the story come out of the Closed Room, Bunning meant to shift to a low spade at trick two, but a high diamond tumbled out of his hand instead. Result: Four spades, doubled, making— +790 Aces.

In the Open Room, South never mentioned spades!

West	North	East	South
Lawrence	Beard	Goldman	Ashburn
1◇	4♠	Pass	Pass
Pass			

Chance. This clever overcall of Beard's had the effect of making South the dummy. From Lawrence's point of view it was surely right to try to cash three rounds of diamonds. Beard ruffed the third and conceded a trick to the ace of spades for +620. However, the damage was already done in the other room where that un-lucky card had "dropped" out of Bunning's hand.

So with one board to go the athletes were leading 3-2. Could my team hang in there for one more board?

Board VI was explosive to say the least.

East-West vul.
Dealer South

                          North
                          ♠ Q J
                          ♡ J 6
                          ◊ K J 9 7 4
                          ♣ 10 9 4 3

West   East
♠ K 9 7 4 3 2   ♠ A 10 8 6 5
♡ 7 5 3 2   ♡ None
◊ None   ◊ 10 8 6 3
♣ K Q 8   ♣ A J 5 2

                          South
                          ♠ None
                          ♡ A K Q 10 9 8 4
                          ◊ A Q 5 2
                          ♣ 7 6

Disaster. In the Closed Room, the bidding, which will serve as a
model for years to come on how to handle distributional hands
after your opponents have exchanged hands, was:

South	West	North	East
Hamman	McCarver	Wolff	Bunning
1♣*	6♠**	7◊***	7♠****
Double*****	Redouble***	Pass	Pass
7 NT*** ****	Double	All Pass	

*Strong and forcing.
**I think I'll keep a little in reserve.
***What the heck, they've seen each others' hands.
****If memory serves me correctly ...
*****Nobody bids a grand slam against one of my club openings.
******Who's he kidding?
*******All right, all right, I believe, I believe.

The defenders cashed the first ten tricks and Hamman was forced to chalk up -1900. (Wolff refused to score such a number.) Now the bidding in the Open Room.

South	West	North	East
Beard	Goldman	Ashburn	Lawrence
5♡	Pass	Pass	Double
Pass	6♠	Double	Pass
Pass	Pass		

Repeat. Ashburn, you see, was still reliving the glory of each of his previous doubles. This one did not exactly turn out to be a success. Goldman casually took the first thirteen tricks while wondering out loud what Ashburn had thought he had seen in his partner's hand. However, the athletes had the last laugh. Six spades doubled, vulnerable, making seven comes to 1860 which was not quite enough to offset the exemplary bidding in the other room. On the other hand if someone had redoubled . . .

Epilogue: In any case "my team" by virtue of straightforward bidding, accurate dummy play, and some remarkable opening leads had managed to defeat the World Champion Aces in a six board match 4-2, proving once and for all that six long peeks are definitely better than four strong Aces.

Me in the World Championships!

This has gone virtually unnoticed until now because of all the attention paid the cheating scandal in Bermuda, but early in the week of the championship I found myself playing one 16 board session against the great Benito Garozzo and Giorgio Belladonna. Yeah, me, Walter Bingham, non-expert. This is how it happened.

The U.S. team and its followers were gathered in the suite of Freddie Sheinwold, the captain, after the first afternoon session against the Italians. From four floors up the sunlight was sparkling on the blue Atlantic Ocean. The players were comparing results and rehashing hands while the rest of us stood around nibbling at the cold cuts Paula Sheinwold had provided. Toward the end of the break, Sheinwold announced that in the second session it would be Bob Hamman and Bob Wolff in the open room, Billy Eisenberg and Eddie Kantar in the closed. Paul Soloway and John Swanson, he said, would have the rest of the afternoon off. Whereupon Nina Swanson said swell, maybe John and Paul would finally take her into Hamilton to shop for sweaters. The way she said it, it sounded more like an order, and off they went.

*The first part of this article was written by Walter Bingham, senior editor and writer for Sports Illustrated. He was covering the World Championship for that magazine as he has done in the past.

As a member of the press, I was entitled to sit in the closed room, so when Eisenberg and Kantar departed, I went with them. As we passed Billy's room, he said he had to make a quick stop and would meet us downstairs.

Eddie and I went to the elevators, pushed the down button and waited. And waited, and waited. I must explain that although the Southampton Princess was in many ways a splendid hotel, its elevators were weird. Mostly they never came. When they did and you got in, the doors would remain open for what seemed like hours. Finally, when those doors decided it was time to close, nothing could stop them, including late-arriving human bodies.

In this case, two strange things happened. The red light for one of the elevators went on, but the doors never opened and eventually the light went off. When we were able to get on one and had pushed the button for the first floor, we sailed right past it, down to the lower lobby. Getting off, we decided it would be more prudent to walk back up.

Garozzo and Belladonna were waiting, along with two monitors to work the bidding screens, a couple of solemn officials of the World Bridge Federation, and a busboy with a tray full of cokes. Benito and Giorgio were seated East and West. Eddie took the North chair. South was for Billy, but Billy had not yet arrived. I drew up a chair behind Eddie. Maurie Braunstein, the tournament director, brought in four boards. We were set, ready for play. But no Billy.

When five minutes had passed and Billy had still not appeared, he was officially late. A phone call to his room produced no answer. The Federation officials were huddled with Maurie Braunstein, trying to decide what to do, when Susan Gunther, the tournament chairman, burst into the room to say that one of the hotel elevators was stuck between the third and second floors. Mechanics had estimated it would take two hours to release the passengers, one of whom was presumably Billy.

In instances where a player is tardy for world championship play, the rules are clear: the third pair may be substituted. Except that in this case the third pair was somewhere in Hamilton trying on shetlands. With Swanson and Soloway unavailable, the

Italians could, if they wanted, accept a forfeit. And who could blame them, since not long before, the U.S. had accused one of its pairs of cheating?

By this time Sandro Salvetti, the Italian captain, was in the room, huddled with Garozzo and Belladonna. Freddie Sheinwold had also appeared. After five minutes the Italians turned to the rest of us in the room and announced their decision. They would not accept a forfeit. Instead they would allow Sheinwold and Kantar to select any partner of their choice, provided that player has no master points to his credit. None. Zero. That ruled out Captain Sheinwold. It ruled out Ozzie Jacoby who was roaming the lobby in his bathing suit. It also ruled out Edgar Kaplan, who might have enjoyed a moment away from the commentator's table; Lew Mathe, just itching for some action, and Dick Frey. It even ruled out Nina, if she had been there. But not me. I was the only person who could tell a heart from a diamond (barely) who did not have a suitcase full of points, red ones, gold ones, whatever. Sheinwold had no choice. He looked at me, shrugged, pointed to the South seat and the game was on.

Kantar speaking now.

I had better take over from Walter to describe this session of sixteen boards. As there was no time to discuss conventions, coupled with the fact that Walter doesn't play any besides Blackwood and Stayman, I figured we had a small survival quotient. (Bigger than if he had played any, however, since the confusion factor was no longer present.)

Besides, I hadn't played strong two bids, grandiose jump overcalls, and cue bids showing first round controls for years. Maybe something good would happen ... by mistake.

I wished I had some way to calm Walter down, as he was obviously nervous. Shaking is actually the proper term. In an earlier session my partner, Billy Eisenberg, had tried to calm me down by lighting up. Unfortunately he lit up a gum wrapper by mistake. I neither smoke nor chew so we were in big trouble.

Fortunately for us the first few hands were rather cut and dry, which means Walter didn't have to be the declarer. Our defense

wasn't exactly first rate, which means we didn't revoke, but I
could see the World Championship vanishing in overtricks alone
if something good didn't happen soon.

Walter was also aware that we weren't taking all of our tricks
on defense and that was adding to his general discomfort. On
board 6 we once again found ourselves on defense. Ugh. (Directions rearranged for reader convenience.)

North-South vul.
Dealer East

```
                        North (Belladonna)
                        ♠ 9 7 5 3 2
                        ♡ K J 7 6
                        ◇ 10 9 4
                        ♣ 3
    West (me)                                    East (Bingham)
    ♠ A J 10 8 4                                 ♠ K Q
    ♡ 9 8 2                                      ♡ A Q 5 4 3
    ◇ J                                          ◇ 7 2
    ♣ A K Q 9                                    ♣ 10 8 7 6
                        South (Garozzo)
                        ♠ 6
                        ♡ 10
                        ◇ A K Q 8 6 5 3
                        ♣ J 5 4 2
```

East	South	West	North
1♡	4◇	4♡	5◇
Pass	Pass	Double	All Pass

Opening lead: K♣

Belladonna had a real problem over 4♡. Should he let Bingham
play a hand when trumps weren't breaking or should he let Bingham and me defend. He had seen our act before so he bid.

Walter was happy to pass 5◇ with his 2½ honor tricks (I forgot
to tell you he still counts that way) and I felt reasonably secure

in doubling even though I too had seen our act before. After all, Walter had opened the bidding and they were vulnerable. What was going on here?

At trick two I hastily shifted to a trump and Bingham nodded, presumably understanding that I was trying to stop club ruffs in dummy.

Garozzo immediately led the ten of hearts and ducked it. Walter, in his haste to play a second trump won the ten with the ace!

Benito naturally placed me with Q x x of hearts, won the trump return in dummy and played the king of hearts discarding a spade and ruffed a heart. Alas, no queen from me and Garozzo had to go down two, taking eight diamonds and a heart. Plus 500 for us. We finally had a good result.

It did not go unnoticed that if Walter had won the ten with the queen Garozzo would later have run the king of hearts through Walter setting up the jack and seven for two discards once the 9-8 both fell.

Looks crossed the table. Walter naturally was apologizing all over the place for "wasting" his ace on declarer's ten as play resumed.

A few more hands, a few more overtricks down the tubes, and then board 9 which caused a bit of a furore.

North-South vul.
Dealer West

                              North (me)
                              ♠ 4 3
                              ♡ Q 10 8 4
                              ◇ A 5 4
                              ♣ A J 8 3

West (Garozzo)   East (Belladonna)
♠ K Q   ♠ 5 2
♡ 9 2   ♡ A J 6 3
◇ K J 10 9 8   ◇ 7 3 2
♣ K Q 7 5   ♣ 10 9 6 4

                              South (Bingham)
                              ♠ A J 10 9 8 7 6
                              ♡ K 7 5
                              ◇ Q 6
                              ♣ 2

West	North	East	South
1◇	Pass	1♡	4♠!
All Pass			

Opening lead: K ♠

It might be pointed out here that Walter's main bridge experience has been on commuter trains to New York each morning. In these games Walter is the big cheese. Consequently he bids quite a bit, as he usually winds up making his contracts against inferior defense.

Meanwhile, back at the table, Benito elected to lead the king of spades, probably thinking that Bingham must have about ten spades and chances of his making two tricks in that suit were close to nil.

Bingham won the ace and exited with the jack, hardly noticing the three or four tricks my dummy had provided for him . . . vulnerable yet!

Garozzo was in trouble. Notice that either red suit lead immediately gives up a trick, and the king of clubs is surely best. Garozzo exited with the even more tricky queen of clubs.

Bingham by now had an advanced case of the jitters. In fact, I wasn't sure but that all his cards would soon be spilling on the table. Besides, he always wanted to grab cards from the dummy instead of calling them.

"Eight of clubs," he finally said. I looked up and played the eight. Bingham was horror-struck. "I mean the ace, I mean the ace" he screamed maniacally. Garozzo and Belladonna looked at each other and then at Bingham pitifully. They didn't want to take advantage, but the director who happened to be in the room at the time ruled that the eight was a played card.

This time Garozzo was in worse shape than before. If he played another club there was no telling which club Bingham would play, but it might be the jack. A diamond might not be safe if Bingham had the queen, and the heart suit looked decidedly unappetizing.

In the end Garozzo exited with the king of diamonds. Bingham looked up. He smiled. He won the ace, discarded a heart on the ace of clubs and said very carefully, "I concede a heart, making four spades, vulnerable."

Play resumed. They bid a cold slam, we naturally let them make seven. They bid a cold game in spades, making six (we were doing better, I led an ace, but we still got squeezed), and finally they stopped in two clubs and we held them to five holding four sure tricks. Nevertheless the match was definitely not out of hand. Between Walter's brilliancies and the overtricks, things were almost even going into the last hand.

North-South vul.
Dealer South

<pre>
                         North (me)
                         ♠ A Q
                         ♡ Q J 10 4
                         ◇ K 4 3 2
                         ♣ A K 5

  West (Garozzo)   East (Belladonna)
  ♠ 10 9 8 7 6   ♠ K J 5 4 2
  ♡ 5   ♡ 8 6 2
  ◇ Q 10 9   ◇ 8 7 6
  ♣ Q J 6 3   ♣ 9 8

                         South (Bingham)
                         ♠ 3
                         ♡ A K 9 7 3
                         ◇ A J 5
                         ♣ 10 7 4 2
</pre>

South	West	North	East
1 ♡	Pass	4 NT	Pass
5 ♡	Pass	5 NT	Pass
6 ◇	Pass	6 ♡	All pass

Even if Walter had both missing kings I wasn't sure I was going to plop him down in seven. The pressure of a vulnerable World Championship grand slam might just be a little too much for him to handle at this point.

In any case 6♡ was the right contract and the ten of spades was led. Walter had no trouble playing the ace as nobody on the commuter trains underleads kings . . . ever.

But just to see who had it, Walter played the queen of spades at trick two and beamed as Belladonna put up the king which was ruffed. I smiled encouragingly. After all so far nothing too terrible had happened.

There was an eerie sort of silence at the table as everyone knew that whatever line of play Walter chose it was unlikely to be duplicated in the other room.

Walter's next move was to play three rounds of hearts leaving the highest heart in dummy. Garozzo parted with two spades.

Now Walter attacked diamonds. He led a diamond to the king, Garozzo playing the ten. Walter eyed that card suspiciously. Could it be a singleton? Perhaps Q-10 doubleton? Obviously it wasn't a singleton or else Garozzo would have started with two red singletons, so it must be Q-10 doubleton! Walter played a diamond to the ace triumphantly. The nine fell. He looked at me. I looked at him. What the hell did he want from me, I was only dummy.

Walter exited with the jack of diamonds to Garozzo's queen. Benito quickly played the jack of clubs to dummy's ace and Belladonna's eight. Walter played the four of diamonds, Belladonna shed a spade and Walter looked at me again. What was it this time I wondered? Didn't he know the four of diamonds was high? Why did I bid so damn much? I'll be an old man before this hand is over, I thought. Finally Walter ruffed and was shattered when Garozzo discarded yet another spade.

"I'm sorry," he muttered, "I just couldn't remember." Silence. Walter turned his attention to the club suit. He remembered earlier that Benito had led a queen from the king-queen and this time he had led the jack. Perhaps he had the queen as well. But what about that distressing eight Belladonna had played. Never mind about that eight. Belladonna was trying to fool him. Nobody fools Bingham, he thought as he crunched the ten of clubs on the table. Garozzo played low unhesitatingly. "Small club," cried Walter. Wonder of wonders, the ten of clubs held, Belladonna's nine came tumbling down and the small slam was made . . . vulnerable. What is more quiet than absolute silence?

As soon as we left the room I started pounding Walter on the back. "Great game," I said. "Let's compare."

We met Sheinwold, Hamman, Wolff, and a bedraggled Eisenberg in room 416 to compare. Four boards were actually pushes. On nine boards we lost small swings almost always due to letting them make overtricks or not making enough tricks when we played the hand. But those nine boards only accounted for 25 IMPS.

On board six where Bingham took the ace of hearts rather than the queen we picked up 7 IMPs because five diamonds doubled went down only one trick in the other room with Hamman declaring.

On board 9 the Italians didn't reach game, stopping in three spades, also making four, so we picked up another 10 IMPs. And finally on board 16 the Italian declarer took the diamond finesse and could no longer make six hearts so we picked up a fat 17 IMPs. We actually won 9 IMPs for the session. Walter was beseiged with warm handshakes. Soloway and Swanson returned from their buying trip with Nina and could hardly believe their ears. Bingham was the hero of the hour.

Then a knock on the door. It was a message from the Italian Captain. It simply said: Per favore, No more Bingham! Sincerely, Sandro Salvetti.

After that you know the story. The Italians, not having to contend with our secret weapon, went on to win the World Championship again, but had they let us use 'the commuter cannon' one more session. . . .

P.S. This entire story is fictional.

The Short Life of the King of Clubs

The world championship in Bermuda two weeks ago was my second. I had played in Rio de Janeiro in 1969, when we finished third, the first time in history the U.S. had not been first or second. That's the story of my life.

But after six days of preliminaries in Bermuda, we were close to victory. We had managed to defeat the French in the semifinals, and in the finals had built a surprising halftime lead of 73 International Match Points against the perennial champions, the Italians. That is like leading the Pittsburgh Steelers 21-0. With only 48 hands left to be played, in segments of 16 each, spirits were soaring. We had a good team, and even though the Italians were capable of playing superb bridge, it would be quite difficult for us to blow this one if we didn't go completely to pot. Could it be? Was I really going to be a world champion?

I had been playing bridge regularly since I learned the game from my best friend's father at the age of 12—30 years ago. Seldom does a day pass that I don't either teach a bridge class, write a bridge column or a bridge article, read about the game, think about the game, dream about the game, bid hands with my partner, deal out hands, or simply play. Was I—that good-for-nothing cardplayer, gambler, bum—finally going to make my worried relatives proud?

So we played 16 hands and dropped 27 of our precious 73-IMP lead, but we went to bed with 46 IMPs still tucked under our pillows. That's a lot. Then 16 more boards the following afternoon and 22 more IMPs disappeared, leaving us 24 IMPs ahead with 16 hands remaining. The Italians had started to play extremely well, better than at any other time during the tournament. Luck, which had been ours, switched sides. Nobody on our team could do anything right.

As I sat down for the last 16 boards I began to reflect upon my errors earlier in the match. I had managed to go down in a vulnerable four spades that I should have made That blew 17 IMPSs. On another hand I thought my partner, Billy Eisenberg, had raised my opening one-club bid to two clubs over an adverse one-diamond overcall, so I had cleverly leaped to five clubs to shut out the opponents' spade fit.

They doubled and set me three tricks when it turned out my right-hand opponent and not Billy had bid the two clubs. Not only that, but Billy had six spades, so they had no makable game. Our other pair, in the meantime, holding the adverse cards, would up playing three notrump, down three. And finally there was my brilliant underlead of the ace-king of hearts over to Billy's queen to get a club ruff. Only Billy didn't have the queen, he had the nine. Expletives resounded.

Our opponents for those last 16 boards on vu-graph (where everyone can witness your atrocities) were those giants of the game, Benito Garozzo and Giorgio Belladonna. This was probably the first time they had ever been down this much going into the last few boards and it didn't amuse them.

Even though Billy and I (especially Billy) were now doing rather well, we felt they had the edge on us—but not 24 IMPs worth. And then it happened: Board 92, a hand that looked as if it might change my life.

North-South vul.
Dealer East

<pre>
                        North
                        ♠ Q J 8
                        ♡ A J 9 6 5
                        ◇ K 8 2
                        ♣ A Q

West   East
♠ 7 6 5 2   ♠ 4 3
♡ K 4 3 2   ♡ Q 10 8 7
◇ J 5 3   ◇ Q 10 6 4
♣ K 10   ♣ 7 5 4

                        South
                        ♠ A K 10 9
                        ◇ None
                        ♡ A 9 7
                        ♣ J 9 8 6 3 2
</pre>

East (Eisenberg)	South (Belladonna)	West (Kantar)	North (Garozzo)
Pass	2♣	Pass	2◇
Pass	2♠	Pass	3♡
Pass	3NT	Pass	4♣
Pass	4◇	Pass	4NT
Pass	5◇	Pass	5♡
Double	Redouble	Pass	5♠
Pass	5NT	Pass	7♣
Pass	Pass	Pass	

Opening lead: 2♡

After Billy passed, Belladonna opened two clubs, which in the Italians' superprecision system showed a long club suit, fewer than 17 high-card points and possibly an outside four-card suit. Garozzo responded two diamonds, a relay, asking for more information, and Belladonna duly bid two spades to show his four-card suit. Garozzo now tried a natural bid of three hearts and Belladonna retreated to three notrump.

Garozzo was far from through; in fact, he was just beginning. He showed his club support by bidding four clubs and Belladonna cue-bid four diamonds, showing either first- or second-round diamond control.

Garozzo made a waiting bid of four notrump (Blackwood is for peasants) and Belladonna confirmed first-round diamond control by bidding five diamonds. Garozzo tried another cue bid of five hearts. Billy, who had seen some of my opening leads, doubled to help me out, and Belladonna seized the opportunity to show first-round heart control by redoubling.

Garozzo bid five spades, a bid whose meaning is not 100% clear to me, and Belladonna bid five notrump, another mystery. Whatever it meant, Garozzo leaped to seven clubs. Everyone passed in exhaustion.

Seven clubs! I could hardly believe my ears. Here I was defending a vulnerable grand slam with the K-10 of trumps tucked away safely in back of the original club bidder. God is not an Italian after all. They were certain to go down one. I was going to be a world champion. What a day. I could hardly wait to get home to tell everybody. I would hold court ... I would ...

I led a heart and then I saw it in the dummy ... the ace-queen doubleton of clubs! Could this really be happening to me? Why me? Why couldn't the ace of trumps be where it should have been? Why couldn't they have dealt Billy the king of clubs? Or why couldn't I have been dealt just one more little club? Just one ... a very little one. Why, why?

Wait. Maybe I did have one. I searched frantically through my spades. The whole scene reminded me of a story I tell my classes. A little old lady, Alice, is playing with a pro, Morris, and she shows out on the second round of hearts, even though Morris knows from the bidding she must have another heart somewhere.

"No hearts, Alice?" he asks. "No hearts, Morris," she replies. "Look in with your diamonds, Alice." "Morris, I have no hearts in with my diamonds." "One more time, please, Alice." "No hearts, Morris." On the last trick Alice rather sheepishly produces a

heart. Morris repeats, "I told you to look in with your diamonds."
"I'm sorry, Morris, it was in with my clubs."

All right, Morris, I'll look through my hearts and my diamonds, I said to myself. (Later at the "victory banquet" I admitted to my teammates that I had searched despairingly through my hand for just one tiny little club, admitting that I would have killed myself if I actually had one and didn't know it. "You wouldn't have had to," said another of the U.S. players, Bob Hamman.)

Meanwhile, upon first viewing dummy, Belladonna thought the big problem was his. He knew he needed to find me with precisely the doubleton king of clubs or possibly the singleton king, in which case an unlikely trump coup was at least feasible. Roughly a 13% chance. He could see the world championship flying out the window. But I knew better; I could see myself flying home with the runner-up trophy.

He ruffed my low heart lead and led a club to the queen, shaking his head. Next he cashed the ace of clubs, and when my king dropped two huge sighs filled the room. One from Belladonna, the other from Billy. We both knew it was all over after that, and so it was.

The last few hands were relatively flat (no swings), and Italy went on to defeat us by 26 IMPs. Had the grand slam been defeated we would have won the match by 3 IMPs. In the closed room, our other pair, Hamman and Bob Wolff, had bid to six no trump, played by North, making seven with a club lead. Admittedly six clubs is the best contract, but six no trump is a far better contract than seven clubs, particularly after North had bid hearts initially, thus inhibiting that most damaging lead.

As soon as the last hand was finished, we were told that Italy had won. The door to the room burst open and a hundred thousand Italians surged in to hug and congratulate the winners.

Billy and I trudged back to our team's rest and recovery room to compare scores and suffer with Hamman-Wolff and Paul Soloway and John Swanson, our other teammates, who must have watched the last 16 boards in horror.

After the comparison there was a long silence. Finally it was broken by Hamman. "This calls for a human sacrifice," he said. I flipped the king of clubs out the terrace window.

Moola at Monte Carlo

Bridge Breaks into the Big Money

If you weren't in Monaco last spring trying to win some of the $60,000 in loot they were giving away at the 1st Annual Bridge Tournament of Monte Carlo, at least make it an attempt to show up next year. You won't be disappointed, that's a promise.

Of course, you should not count on winning either the five-session open pair game or the team game if the Italians show up. But second place in the pair game pays $5,000 and the $2,500 that the Americans Sontag and Weichsel picked up for coming in third was not so bad either. (Ogust-Koytchou finished sixth.)

However, do not despair. The rules do not allow Garozzo and Belladonna to play together in the Mixed Pairs and plenty of francs are available in that event also.

I played in the pair game with Billy Eisenberg, and if they had just stopped the fight after four sessions when we were in second place I would have been a rich man. However, the rules called for a fifth session and when the smoke cleared we were a distant 15th which was good for a letdown and $500.

The language barrier was evident from the start. The French wanted to bid in French (the nerve), the Italians in Italian, and the English and particularly the Americans in English.

Instead of discussing conventions when you came to the table you worked out which language would be used. This, in addition to the French cards where the jacks and kings, not to mention the queens, look quite a bit alike, also led to a bit of difficulty.

Billy even accussed me of dogging it when I refused to capture dummy's king of spades with my queen. He, in turn, was trying desperately to bid in French. His "un's" (which mean one in French) always sounded to me like someone who needed an enema. His command of the language broke down completely on this deal:

East-West vul.
Dealer East

                    North
                    ♠ J 9 4
                    ♡ A 7 6
                    ◇ J 8 5
                    ♣ A 10 7 6

West   **East**
♠ 8 2   ♠ K Q 10 6 5
♡ K Q J 10 9 8 3 2   ♡ 5
◇ None   ◇ 7 4 2
♣ J 5 4   ♣ K 9 3 2

                    South
                    ♠ A 7 3
                    ♡ 4
                    ◇ A K Q 10 9 6 3
                    ♣ Q 8

After East passed, Billy opened the South hand with un carreau (one diamond), West volunteered trois coeurs (three hearts) to which I said contre (double). Billy now decided to make the brilliant rebid of three notrump which in French is trois sans atout. But in his excitement of having no heart stop it came out trois sans atois. Even so it was a brilliant bid.

He won the second heart and ran seven diamonds reducing all hands to four cards. When East came down to two cards in each black suit he was thrown in with a spade and forced to lead a club.

Billy guessed the position and made five notrump for a big score. (298 is top on a board.)

A contract of six diamonds is not without interest. Say a heart is led to the ace and a low club led from dummy at trick two. East must play low. After South wins the queen he draws trump and ducks a spade. East must return a club to break up a double squeeze.

And now a lesson hand, also from the Pair Game.

Both sides vul.
Dealer East

```
                    North
                    ♠ 10 9 5
                    ♡ A K 8 5
                    ◇ A 6 5
                    ♣ A 8 2
     West                              East
     ♠ K Q J 7                         ♠ 8 6 4
     ♡ 9 4                             ♡ Q J 10 3
     ◇ J 10 7                          ◇ K 8 2
     ♣ J 10 7 5                        ♣ Q 6 4
                    South
                    ♠ A 3 2
                    ♡ 7 6 2
                    ◇ Q 9 4 3
                    ♣ K 9 3
```

After North opens fourth seat with either one club or one heart, South plays one notrump. West, of course, leads the king of spades.

South wins the third spade and leads a low diamond to dummy's ace. West should play the ten or the jack. This increases South's options in the diamond suit. If he, in fact, leads back to his nine of diamonds or ducks the second round completely, playing West for either K 10 or K J doubleton, the defenders come to one additional trick. At the tables where West sleepily played the seven, declarer played right back to his queen to take three diamonds and eight tricks in all.

Omar Sharif came up with this beautifully played hand from the Team Game.

Neither side vul.
Dealer North

$$\text{North}$$
♠ A K Q 2
♡ J 8 3
◊ 10 5 4
♣ K 6 3

West
♠ J 9 7 4
♡ K 9 6 4 2
◊ J 9 6 3
♣ None

East
♠ 10 8 5
♡ 10
◊ A 8 2
♣ A Q J 10 9 7

South
♠ 6 3
♡ A Q 7 5
◊ K Q 7
♣ 8 5 4 2

North	East	South	West
1♣	Pass*	1♡	Pass
1♠	Pass	2 NT	Pass
3 NT	Pass**	Pass	Pass

*Asking about the club bid.
**Asking again about the club bid.
Opening lead: 3◊

If the rules had permitted, West would have gone to the store to buy a club to lead after the interrogation East put Omar through. However, East's acute desire for a club lead (without risking a double, of course) cost him dearly in the end.

Omar put up the ten of diamonds which East ducked hoping to preserve his entry to his precious clubs. Omar now led a low heart to the queen and king and West exited with a diamond to East who finally won his ace and returned the suit.

A heart was led to dummy's eight and three top spades were cashed leaving this position:

North
♠ 2
♡ J
♢ None
♣ K 6 3

West   **East**
♠ J   **♠ None**
♡ 9 6 4   **♡ None**
♢ J   **♢ None**
♣ None   **♣ A Q J 10 9**

South
♠ None
♡ A 7
♢ None
♣ 8 5 4

Omar needed three of the last five tricks. He led a club from dummy to East's nine, as West discarded a heart. East now cashed his ace of clubs and led a third club squeezing West in the majors.

If East returns a club to the king instead of cashing the ace, Omar wins the king cashes dummy's jack of hearts and leads the deuce of spades to West's jack. West must return a heart (he was forced to discard his diamond earlier) and Omar makes his ninth trick with his stranded ace of hearts.

Do you think you and your favorite partner could get to seven spades or notrump after West deals and opens one notrump? These are the East-West hands.

West
♠ 9 7 4 2
♡ A K J 6
♢ A Q 3
♣ K 6

East
♠ A K Q 8 3
♡ Q 9 7
♢ 10 6
♣ A Q 5

The great bidders all got to seven but the really great bidders stopped in six. You see South had all four of the missing spades.

And now the highlight of the tournament for me.

North-South vul.
Dealer East.

                        North
                        ♠ A 5 4
                        ♡ 10 8 5 4
                        ♢ 6 5
                        ♣ J 6 4 3

West   **East**
♠ J 7   ♠ K Q 10 8 3 2
♡ K J 9 3   ♡ A Q 7
♢ 10 9 3   ♢ 7 4 2
♣ A K Q 5   ♣ 9

                        South
                        ♠ 9 6
                        ♡ 6 2
                        ♢ A K Q J 8
                        ♣ 10 8 7 2

East opened one spade and I glanced at my opponents convention card to see whether or not they were playing negative doubles. I always overcall on less if they are.

Well, they had "Sputnik" written down and I was told earlier that in France that is the equivalent of a negative double. So I overcalled 2 D, West doubled and naturally everyone passed and there I was.

Another well conceived overcall. They have no game and they can beat me 500 without working up a sweat. Oh yes, there is one thing I forgot to mention. I was playing against two emotional French experts, one of whom, East, had just given up smoking the day before. (This becomes relevant.)

West started out with the ace of clubs and I could just see my match point score of 3 out of a possible 298 come rolling in. In spite of East's nine West shifted to the jack of spades.

Now, I could at least get out for one down if I won the ace and drew trumps and set up a seventh trick in clubs. But I visualized a bad trump break and a probable 3-2 club division so I ducked the spade. East ground the deuce of spades into the table as if it were really his last cigarette, but West, undaunted, continued the suit giving me one more chance to draw trumps. Not me. I led a low club from dummy and East immediately ruffed with the four of diamonds — but West didn't see it and put the queen of clubs on the trick.

The stage was now set. East knew it was his lead but West thought it was his. They both played their black kings at the same time. I decided to accept East's lead and ruffed it as West was now forced to put his king of clubs on the trick. Now, I made my contract. But that was not the end of it.

East and West started to talk to each other in very fast French. Finally, they both got up from the table and put their noses in each other's faces. Even the arbitre (director, stupid) couldn't pull them part. Finally, East came over to apologize and said he had just given up smoking and was very nervous. And all the time I thought it was West's fault.

Now for the low point. In the Team Game, Billy and I teamed up with Robert Sheehan and Irving Rose from Great Britain. In order to get into the money you must qualify first in your section. There are eight sections and about twenty teams in each section. We just missed qualifying and played in the consolation Swiss Team Event.

With two matches to go we were tied for first and Billy and I sat down to play against former World Champions Pabis-Ticci and D'Alelio.

As I was sorting my cards, Terence Reese pulled up a chair in back of me. He was on a six man team and apparently was not playing this match. Well, I thought to myself, I'll show Terence a thing or two. Especially since he and his partner, John Collings, had given us two bad boards in our disastrous fifth session of the Pair Game.

This was my hand, second to speak, with neither side vulnerable:

♠ J 5 4   ♡ A 6 5 4   ◇ A Q 5   ♣ A K 10

Pabis-Ticci to my right passed and I opened one club. Billy responded one diamond and just as I was about to say two notrump, Pabis-Ticci overcalled one spade. What to do?

One notrump was out; two no trump without a spade stopper wasn't appealing; a reverse to two hearts with only three clubs is not my style. So I bid what I see all the experts in the bidding contests bid. When they don't know what to do, they cue bid the opponent's suit and then blame their partner for anything that goes wrong. So I bid a smart two spades.

Billy now took me back to three clubs which I corrected to three diamonds. Boy, was I showing Terence a thing or two about bidding. Now Billy bid three hearts. What the hell was this? One thing was for sure. We had no spade stopper so three notrump was out. Billy and I were still good friends so I discounted three spades and raised to four hearts. Now, I had actually done what I had been accusing Lew Mathe of doing for years. I had bid all four suits with a balanced hand!

Billy now bid five clubs, and exhausted from this complicated yet precise auction I passed. A spade was led and these were the two hands in all their glory:

North
♠ 9 3 2
♡ Q 7 3
◇ K 10 4 2
♣ J 4 3

South
♠ J 5 4
♡ A 6 5 4
◇ A Q 5
♣ A K 10

As Pabis-Ticci cashed three spades I saw Terence going for his
pencil and notebook. West discarded a heart on the third spade
and East shifted to a heart which I ducked to West's king. I won
the heart return in dummy and tried to avoid a heart ruff by playing three rounds of clubs, West winning the queen. West exited
with a diamond, and after I cashed two rounds of diamonds, East
spread his hand and claimed the balance with the long trump and
two more good spades. Down six!

Terence Reese or no Terence Reese, I am still going back to this
tournament organized so beautifully by the French International-
ist Jean-Michel Boulenger and run so well by Harold Franklin
of England.

P.S. We lost the Swiss Team Match, but America's honor was
salvaged when the event was won by Peter Weichsel, Alan Sontag, Gene Neiger, Hal Fein and lovely Nancy Weichsel.

The Answering Service

When my phone rings and I answer it with an expectant "hello," I am secretly wishing that a soft feminine voice will be on the other end. Second choice is a close friend (any sex) and third is good news (from anyone).

Alas, what I usually get on the other end is not a hello (from either sex) but a bridge hand. And these calls can come at some very strange hours, let me assure you.

At first I was flattered that someone considered my opinion so valuable that I would be chosen to settle an argument.

However, it soon became aparent that it wasn't my bid that was wanted, but rather an approval of the bid that the caller made; or more likely, a display of disgust at the bid made by the caller's partner.

Not only that, but the caller has a way of "leaning" me towards the bid he wants to hear.

For example:

Me: "Hello."

Caller: "You hold: K-J-x-x-x-, x, A-Q-x-x, Q-x-x."

Me: (Groggy) "O.K."

Caller: "You open one spade, partner bids two clubs, you bid two diamonds, partner two hearts, you three clubs, and partner four spades. You wouldn't dream of passing, would you?"

117

Translation: either the caller held this hand, bid, and parter got very upset, or caller's partner held the hand, passed, and a slam was missed. In any case, I know that it is right to bid on, even though I wouldn't know for sure what to do if I actually held the hand.

Me: "What, pass at this point? Surely you must be joking. Who in the world ever did that?" By now, of course, the caller loves me and is glad that he woke me up. Worse, he will call again.

Then, of course there are the calls that don't come with any early clues about what to bid. As you think, the caller becomes frantic. Maybe you will actually agree with his hated partner! Little hints start filtering in.

Let's say that he has given me the above hand without any intonations, and I am thinking. Just as I am about to pass I hear, "Looks like at least a small slam, maybe even a grand if partner has the right cards, right?"

"Well," I mumble, and then finding my backbone I say, "No, I can't imagine passing. I was just thinking what the best road was to either a small or a grand slam."

Then, of course, there is the call from the friendly player who has just made a master bid so subtle that not even Garozzo, Belladonna and Forquet all lumped together would have thought of it.

If the "master bid" hasn't worked because partner simply couldn't cope with such a brilliancy, you are given a subtle push towards the bid, coaxing you into the same horrible quagmire.

Worse, if the bid has worked there is absolute silence on the other end as the caller is hoping (praying) you don't make the same bid so that he can describe it in all its glory. Example:

Me: "Hello."

Caller: "You have x-x-x, x-x, A-J-x-x-x-x, x-x."

Me: (Groggy) "Huh?"

Caller: "Wake up! Your right hand opponent opens one club, you pass, LHO says two clubs, partner overcalls two hearts, 2 NT on your right, passed around to partner who doubles. This is passed around to your LHO who retreats to three clubs and this is passed around to you. What do you do?"

The bidding:

East	South	West	North
1♣	Pass	2♣	2♡
2 NT	Pass	Pass	Double
Pass	Pass	3♣	Pass
Pass	??		

Silently I wait for some help. What does she want from me now? Let me review the conversation. Do the words "retreats to three clubs" have any special significance? Is this the time for an inferential double? Even I am smart enough to know that bidding diamonds (the obvious move) can't be right, or else why the call in the middle of the night?

I have a few moves of my own when I need to stall for time and perhaps get an extra clue or two.

Me: "What's the vulnerability?" (A very good stall)

Caller: "Both vulnerable, what do you bid?" (I can see this is the "brilliancy" bid and I am not going to get any further help. Nevertheless . . .)

Me: "Who am I playing with?"

Caller: "A very good player." (This is to let me know that they play with good partners, which is another round-a-bout way of telling me that they too are pretty darn good.)

Me: "Duplicate or IMPs?" (Desperation setting in.)

Caller: "Duplicate, come on."

Me: "Do we have any agreements I should know about?" (Clearly, I'm in big trouble now.)

Caller: "No, you must work it all out for youself."

Me: "Did I play in this event? The hands looks very familiar." (Obviously, it's all over for me. They are going to begin the count any second.)

Caller: "No. It happened tonight."

Me: "Oh."

Caller: "So what do you bid?"

Me: "What do I bid?"

Caller: "Yes."

Me: (End of the rope) "I bid 3 ◊."

Caller: Silence.

Me: (Speaking faster) "What am I supposed to do, double? Does my partner have a singleton diamond or something? If he has six hearts he can correct." (Foaming) "Don't tell me I am supposed to bid three hearts. Maybe I should just pass."

Caller: Silence.

Me: (Frantic) "What did you do?"

Caller: "Can't you see, it is so obvious."

Me: "Of course, it is obvious but what did you do just for the heck of it?"

Caller: (Triumphantly) "I bid three notrump."

Me: "You what?"

Caller: "I bid three notrump. I was sure you would too. Obviously partner has a strong hand with a club stopper, and he can't have too many clubs with all this club bidding on my left, so he must have some diamonds. If that is the case I thought I could bring in three notrump. Want to know my partner's hand?

Me: (Crushed) "Please."

Caller: (Speaking louder all the time) "Partner had: A-J-x, A-Q-x-x-x, K-10-x, A-x. I finessed the notrump bidder for Q-x-x of diamonds and we got a cold top."

Me: "Really, a cold top for three notrump. It looks like such an obvious contract. My partner would have bid 3 NT over my 3 ◊."

Caller: "Oh no he wouldn't! He would have played me for a weaker diamond suit. He even told me so. Now I have another one where I made an even better bid."

Me: "Spare me. Please tell me about it tomorrow. I need a day to think about your last bid."

Caller: "O.K. Talk to you tomorrow." Click.

(Dear God, what have I ever done to deserve this?)

I Once Had a Friend —
Her Name Was Amalya

Before my kibitzer, Amalya Kearse, tells one more person about what I did on that hand from the final session of the Blue Ribbon Pairs, I will tell it myself.

At the time of "the incident" I was playing — and I use the verb rather loosely — with Alan Sontag.

At one point in time during this six-session event we were within one point of the lead. By the time the event ended, it would have taken a high-powered microscope to find our names on the list of finishers.

During the course of the fifth session "the hand" took place. It was a fairly ordinary looking hand:

♠A Q 8 ♡Q 9 7 ◊K ♣J 9 7 5 3 2

— but one I sort of liked.

My left hand opponent (I made a blood oath with my opponents not to mention names in this deal — you'll see why later) opened 1 NT. Not being the curious type, I didn't bother to look at his convention card. If I had, I would have seen that they were playing a "mini notrump", 9-12 points. Why bother with details? My partner overcalled 2♣, Landy, asking for the majors, and there was a pass to my right.

121

What to bid? A "normal" Landy is supposed to have 5-5 in the majors, but I have seen that whittled down to 5-4, 4-4, and even 4-3 by some real perverts.

In any case, if Alan had one five-card major and one four-card major, I wanted to play in the 5-3 fit. We hadn't discussed this, so I gambled that 3♣ would be forcing, hopefully asking for his longer major.

This response was greeted by good news and bad news. The good news was that Alan didn't pass. The bad news was that he bid 3◇ , a bid that didn't ring clear at the time.

In any case I bid 3♡ and Alan raised to four. My left hand opponent led a small diamond and Alan spread his "Landy" on the table:

♠ 10 9 3 2
♡ K J 3 2
◇ A J 5 4
♣ A

♠ A Q 8
♡ Q 9 7
◇ K
♣ J 9 7 5 3 2

Well, I've seen better but I've also seen much worse. My immediate problem was finding 10 tricks, keeping in mind, of course, that I was under the delusion that West had a strong notrump.

On hands like this that seem to involve crossruffing, I have the habit of playing out the hand mentally and moving the cards over in my hand physically to see what my hand will look like after about six or seven tricks. I didn't like what I saw, but there was a time limit and the director was hovering about (from previous slow play at our table), so I decided to plunge in and hope for the best.

I won the ◇ K, crossed to the ♣A (my last proper play) as West contributed the ♣Q. I cashed the ◇ A, discarding a spade (mistake number one) and went to ruff a diamond. I went to ruff it, that is, but they told me I could not ruff it with the ♣3—the card that I had actually deposited on the third round of diamonds. Hearts were trump, I was reminded by Alan, not clubs.

As it turned out, East won the third round of diamonds and played the ♡A [*where did he get that card?*] and another heart.

I played the nine on the second heart, and won the jack when West covered. I now ruffed the ◊ J back to my hand with the bare ♡ Q, everyone following. At this point, having lost two tricks, my position was:

♠ 10 9 3 2
♡ K 3
◊ None
♣ None

♠ A Q
♡ None
◊ None
♣ J 9 7 5

I led a low club and when West played the king, I must have had conflicting thoughts to account for what I was about to do. I must have thought that (1) my clubs were now good and I could not get back to them, (2) that trumps were not breaking 3-3 and perhaps I could force West to play a spade into my major tenace.

In any case I ruffed high and exited with a low trump, West winning, both following, as I discarded a club.

At this point I knew West had only spades and I claimed! This was probably my best play in the entire hand (tournament?) as my opponents who had never seen a hand played quite like this, accepted!

It was only on the next round after I had settled back to the applause of the other kibitzers, smugly thinking I had somehow rectified the count by unwittingly pitching a club instead of ruffing, and had further "brilliantized" the play by ruffing high to force the spade lead, that Amalya leaned over and asked me, "Didn't East have the guarded ♣10 in the end position?"

It was only then that it dawned on me what I had done. Furthermore, Amalya told me another kibitzer had leaned over to her and whispered, "Wasn't that a brilliantly played hand?"

It was obvious to me at this moment that Amalya would have to be bought off. But how? And how much? As I was mulling this problem over between sessions I could see that it was already too late. She had written the hand down and was showing it to everybody, and I mean everybody.

So before Amalya comes up to you with the entire hand plus the story of my "fake ruff" followed by my "fake claim", let me show you all four hands. It happens to be a lovely hand after all, Amalya.

North
♠ 10 9 3 2
♡ K J 3 2
◇ A J 5 4
♣ A

West
♠ K J 7 6
♡ 10 8 6
◇ Q 8 6 2
♣ K Q

East
♠ 5 4
♡ A 5 4
◇ 10 9 7 3
♣ 10 8 6 4

South
♠ A Q 8
♡ Q 9 7
◇ K
♣ J 9 7 5 3 2

Proper play is to cash the ♣A at trick two, discard a *club* on the ◇ A and *ruff* a low diamond. Next a club is ruffed in dummy low, followed by a ruff of the ◇ J. At this point, declarer exits with the ♡ Q, six tricks in hand. If East ducks, declarer ruffs two more clubs in dummy along with the ♠A for 10 tricks, so East must win.

East must return a spade and declarer plays the queen, losing to the king. At this point West does best to return the ♠J, locking declarer in his hand. No matter.

When declarer leads a spade, East ruffs, but that's the defender's last trick. So what's all the fuss, Amalya? The hand was always cold.

The Best Hands From The Salt Lake City Nationals

A View From the Top by a Winner of the Grand National

Now that I am home and all my bad bids and plays are well behind me, I can review the most recent National Championship.

Salt Lake City really was a splendid city to host a National Tournament. The Salt Palace had excellent facilities, the weather was great, the city was clean and, personally, I only heard compliments about the whole tournament. More Nationals in Salt Lake City.

Then I heard this story from Soloway before the Nationals started. It seems that he and Bobby Goldman were practicing for Salt Lake City by playing in a Regional Knockout in Fort Worth. Paul picked up his hand:

♠Q J x x ♡K Q x x x ◇Q J x ♣x

He couldn't resist opening two diamonds, Flannery. Goldman responded 3♠, holding:

♠A K x x x x ♡— ◇A K x x ♣x x x

The way this pair plays, 3♠ is forcing and compels cue bidding by the opener. Paul knew he was supposed to bid 4♣ but he couldn't get himself to do it. He rebid four spades.

Undaunted, Goldman tried once more with 5♢. Again Paul could not get himself to do anything with his trashy Flannery but bid 5♠. Goldman finally passed.

After six was made not a word was said. Later they went to dinner, and as Paul glanced down the menu he saw a dish entitled "Chicken Flannery". He ordered it.

One more story before the hands. One of the evenings, there was a Goren bidding panel show moderated by Harold Ogust.

Questions were asked from the audience, directed at various members of the panel. The time was about one-in-the-morning.

Finally, one lady raised her hand and was recognized by Harold. She said she noticed that so many people were attending these shows, couldn't some of them stay afterwards, perhaps til about 2 a.m., and form a quorum for a membership meeting?

Harold said that this type of question was not quite in line with the spirit of the show, but he would take a poll to see how many were interested in staying around for the proposed membership meeting.

As about four people raised their hands to stay and about 300 did not, the issue was settled. The very next question was this: "If the bidding goes 2 NT, pass, pass, should you double?"

Jim Jacoby fielded this one: Anyone, he said, who would double two notrump on that auction, would also vote to attend the membership meeting at 2 a.m. Amen.

Unfortunately, the few hands that I have may not be as good as the stories, but you can't have everything.

My old partner and good friend, Marshall Miles, is the "star" of the first hand. He accomplished something that is seldom seen at the bridge table—he went down nine tricks undoubled in a voluntarily bid three notrump!

East-West vul.
Dealer East

                        North
                        ♠ K x
                        ♡ J x
                        ◇ x x x
                        ♣ K Q J x x x

West   **East**
♠ J x   ♠ A Q 10 x x x
♡ A Q x x x x x   ♡ x x
◇ K x   ◇ 10 x x
♣ x x   ♣ x x

                        South
                        ♠ x x x
                        ♡ K 10
                        ◇ A Q J x x
                        ♣ A 10 x

East	South	West	North
Pass	1◇	2♡	3♣
Pass	3 NT	All Pass	

Seems reasonably normal, doesn't it? Well, it was until West led the jack of spades. East rattled off six spade tricks and West hung on to every one of his bloody hearts. When East shifted to a heart, West took the last seven tricks.

Everything happens to Marshall.

Although I can't top Marshall's story, I can come close. Many years ago I wrote an article for the Bridge World asking if perhaps I hadn't set a record by going down one in 3 NT with 31 high card points between the two hands and all suits doubly stopped.

I made a great effort to break that record in a losing quarterfinal match against the Rapee team in the Spingold when I managed to come up with 8 tricks in a contract of 4 NT, again with 31 high card points between the two hands.

Neither side vul.
Dealer South

                         North
                         ♠ K x x
                         ♡ A x x x
                         ◇ x x
                         ♣ K J x x

West   East
♠ Q 10 9   ♠ x x x x
♡ Q 10   ♡ 9 8 x x
◇ J 10 9 x x x x   ◇ Q
♣ x   ♣ Q 10 9 8

                         South
                         ♠ A J x
                         ♡ K J x
                         ◇ A K x
                         ♣ A x x x

South	West	North	East
2 NT	Pass	3 ♣	Pass
3 ◇	Pass	4 NT	All pass

Opening lead: J ◇

Actually this hand is going to prove even more embarrassing
than I thought. As I look it over I see that I had the ace-king
of every suit, three suits in which there were finesses, and a seven
and an eight card fit to work with. With all that I only took the
four aces and the four kings!

John Solodar led the jack of diamonds and I allowed George
Rapee's queen to hold. (A very doubtful play, but I had my reasons. Just don't ask me what they were.)

Rapee switched to a spade and I played low, winning the nine
with the king. I led a heart to the jack and queen and won the
heart return with the king.

I cashed a diamond and George shed a spade. Next I tried the
ace and a club, ducking when West showed out. (This was also

not so clever, as a low club to the jack would have kept open more squeeze possibilities — for down one.)

East shifted to a spade and my jack lost to the queen. As there was no way to avoid the loss of still another trick I was down two.

At the other table after a one club opening by South, a 3 ◊ overcall by West, and a negative double by North, they stopped miraculously at three notrump and made it on an end play.

And finally a hand from the Life Master's Pairs. In this event I played for the first time with Alan Sontag of New York.

Alan is a great natural bridge player and seldom errs. However, in an effort to play the way I like, he tried desperately to learn my method of signalling and discarding to show both count, suit preference and attitude.

The fact that it is too complicated for me, added to the fact that I didn't explain it very well, finally did us in.

Briefly (I can just hear Alan saying to himself, "Oh no"), if you are discarding, your first card is attitude. The next card is count. If it is close in number to the first card it shows an even number, if it is far apart from the first card it shows an odd number.

Therefore, the deuce followed by the three means that you don't like the suit with an even number of cards, but the deuce followed by the eight means that you don't like it with an odd number of cards. The same is true with a high-low.

A high-low such as the three-deuce means you like the suit and have an even number of cards, and a high-low such as the eight-deuce means that you like the suit with an odd number of cards.

In order to help Alan remember this, I told him the key words "not even close" (forget the not) and "far out," substitute odd for out.

Of course, these signals did not apply when partner leads the suit first or you lead the suit first. Only when discarding.

I should have known we were in trouble when I heard Alan mumbling "close apart" after one of our discussions.

Just to show you that I can finally do any great player in (I can see Billy nodding his head) this is what happened.

North-South vul.
Dealer North

<pre>
                        North
                        ♠ A 9 8 x x
                        ♡ A x
                        ◇ A Q x x
                        ♣ x x

West   East
♠ J x x   ♠ Q x
♡ x x x x   ♡ K J 9 x
◇ x x   ◇ x
♣ Q 10 x x   ♣ A K J 9 x 2

                        South
                        ♠ K 10 x
                        ♡ Q 10 x
                        ◇ K J 10 x x x
                        ♣ x
</pre>

North	East	South	West
1♠	2♣	2◇	4♣
4◇	5♣	5◇	All Pass

Opening lead: Q♣

Clearly, I should have bid four hearts over four diamonds, but I didn't.

After Alan made this great opening lead, I played the deuce trying to get a shift to hearts.

If it hadn't been for those interminable count discussions Alan would have played a heart like a flash at trick two. But he finally got to thinking I had five clubs and continued the suit. So they made five diamonds and Alan left the table hating himself.

However, there was both good and amazing news to report after this, the last hand of the event.

The good news was that we achieved almost as good a score for letting them make five diamonds as we would have for defeating them because most of the field was in four spades, making.

The amazing news was that Alan wanted to try it again in Pittsburgh.

The Biggest Set of the Year!

Down 3200 Points! — Is It Possible?

Shortly after returning from the National Championships in Atlanta, my good friend and former partner, Marshall Miles, came over to hear "all about the hands."

Just as I was about to launch into all my stories, particularly reasons for all my "unlucky" bids and plays, Marshall very casually asked, "Did you hear about the 3200 set?"

I stopped short. "What did you say?" Marshall repeated, "Oh, nothing much, just that there was a 3200 set recently in the nickel game." (Translation — a $160.00 hand.)

"Marshall, if there was a 3200 point set you must have been in on it, and I can't tell from your face whether you were on the right or wrong side." Marshall smiled. "O.K., so you were on the right side, but don't torture me any longer, tell me about the hand."

"Well," Marshall began, "I was sitting West and I picked up:

♠ — ♡ A K Q 3 ◇ K J 7 6 5 ♣ A K Q 4.

I opened the bidding with 2♣ (artificial) and this is how the bidding proceeded:

West	North	East	South
2♣	Pass	2♠	Pass
3◇	Pass	4◇	Pass
?			

"Now, what would you bid?" "Five no trump, the Grand Slam Force," I replied. "Right on." (Already, I knew some great transformation had taken place in Marshall because he had never used that expression before.)

"Your partner leaps to seven diamonds to show two of the top three honors and your right hand opponent doubles, probably asking for a spade lead." "So you redoubled, is that how you made 3200 points?" "No, that would have only come to 2610, and I was shooting for a big score." "So what did you do?" "I redoubled." "And?"

"The fellow that doubled, South, decided he couldn't set me after all and ran to seven hearts! I tried not to double too loudly but they tell me that I shattered seven windows, but it doesn't matter I can afford to have them replaced."

"Will you please show me the hand? Please."

North
♠ Q 5 4
♡ 4 2
◇ 9 4 3
♣ J 10 7 6 3

West
♠ None
♡ A K Q 3
◇ K J 7 6 5
♣ A K Q 4

East
♠ K J 9 8 7
♡ 6 5
◇ A Q 10 2
♣ 9 5

South
♠ A 10 6 3 2
♡ J 10 9 8 7
◇ 8
♣ 8 2

The entire bidding:

West	North	East	South
2♣	Pass	2♠	Pass
3◇	Pass	4◇	Pass
5 NT	Pass	7◇	Double
Redouble	Pass	Pass	7♡
Seven-Window — All Pass			
Double			

"What did you lead, Marshall?" "I led the queen of hearts." "Marshall, you are so tricky, did it hold?" "Fortunately, and then I shifted to the queen of clubs." "Marshall, you are such a showoff." "Anyway, I continued with the ace and a low club which my partner ruffed and declarer overtrumped. Wiggle as he might, he could not take more than two trump tricks and went down eleven, which amounted to 3200 points."

"Was there complete silence at the table after the hand was over?" "Oh no, the dummy was sure that if his partner hadn't played so carelessly he could have held it to down ten!"

Picking North America's Team

The Best Hands of the Houston Play-Offs

The setting for the 1977 U.S. Team Trials, January 5-9, was the third floor of the Shamrock Hilton Hotel in Houston.

Three teams were poised and ready to play. Briefly, the situation was this: The Rosenkranz team (Dr. George Rosenkranz, Roger Bates, John Mohan, Dr. Richard Katz, Larry Cohen) had won both the Vanderbilt and the Spingold the preceding year and had thus earned a bye into the finals. The Reisinger winners (Ira Rubin, Fred Hamilton, Eric Paulsen, Hugh Ross, with the addition of Mike Passell and Ron Von der Porten) would play the Grand National winners (John Swanson, Paul Soloway, Billy Eisenberg, Eddie Kantar, with the addition of Bob Wolff and Bob Hamman) in a 128 board semi-final match. Non-playing captains were John Gerber (Rosenkranz), Dan Morse (Reisinger) and Roger Stern (Grand Nationals).

Our team went to Dallas two days before the trials to get in a little practice against the local heroes. Paul Soloway was already in good form.

Soloway, South, opened one notrump and then became declarer in six notrump. Yes, six clubs is easier, but Swanson figured Paul needed the practice.

North
- ♠ J 4
- ♡ A K
- ◇ J 10 8 3
- ♣ A K 10 6 5

West
- ♠ 8 6
- ♡ 9 5 4
- ◇ Q 9 7 4 2
- ♣ 9 3 2

East
- ♠ Q 10 9 7 2
- ♡ Q 10 8 3
- ◇ K 6
- ♣ 8 4

South
- ♠ A K 5 3
- ♡ J 7 6 2
- ◇ A 5
- ♣ Q J 7

West led a heart, East signalling with the eight, and the jack of diamonds was covered and taken by the ace. A diamond was returned, dummy's eight spot holding, and then came the club avalanche, burying East at the pass. This was the position as the last club was about to be played:

North
- ♠ J 4
- ♡ A
- ◇ 10 3
- ♣ 10

West
- ♠ 8 6
- ♡ 9 5
- ◇ Q 9
- ♣ None

East
- ♠ Q 10 9 7
- ♡ Q 10
- ◇ None
- ♣ None

South
- ♠ A K 5 3
- ♡ J 7
- ◇ None
- ♣ None

On the last club, East parted with a spade, declarer a heart, and West also a heart. The jack of spades was led, and when East covered, he was allowed to hold the trick and now Soloway had the rest.

A minus-one squeeze, not a bad way to get started.

Just before we left for Houston, Hamman and Wolff wanted to play a little two cent set rubber bridge game against Billy and me. We accepted.

Holding a little over two thirds of the cards, Billy and I managed to hold our losses to $90.00 each. All this in spite of the warnings of our captain, Roger Stern, about playing these intra-squad set-games for money. In any case, our morale after that drubbing was so high that Billy drove to Houston with some of the other guys and I flew.

That is, I tried to fly. Roger, his wife Sandy, and I had reservations on a 6 P.M. Tuesday flight from Love Airport which is a bit out of the city.

When we get there they tell us the flight is delayed until 7, and at 7 they tell us the flight is cancelled. Now we have to get back to the Dallas-Fort Worth airport and try to make either a 7:30 (standby) or an 8:30 flight to Houston.

We get there just in time to get on the 7:30, but it doesn't leave until 8:15. At last we are flying to Houston. But what's this? Just as we arrive over the city the captain announces that due to the fog the plane cannot land, but it will circle over Houston until it can.

That doesn't sound too bad. But an hour later, as we are still circling, the captain announces that we cannot land and that we are going back to Dallas. %!&*$!!. Those weren't my exact feelings, but this is a family magazine.

Just before we are about to land in Dallas (it is about 10:45 PM and I have to play the next day) the captain announces that it has cleared up in Houston and they are preparing another plane for those of us who still want to go. Fine. We wait around the airport until another announcement is made. No flight to Houston that evening, period. &*!%$†)*&! and then some.

So now what? It is about 11:30 and I'm getting tired and we are all hungry. Of course, nothing is open at the airport. Oh, to be back in civilization again.

Roger gets the brilliant idea of renting a car. After all, it is only a four hour drive when you can see the road, so why not go when you can't and make it more interesting?

We do it. We get a Hertz car (sorry Avis), stop for something to eat, and begin the journey at about midnight.

I am the honored guest so I get the back seat all to myself. I am supposed to sleep. It is hard for me to sleep when I am supposed to, and besides I have long legs and no place to put them, but I try.

Roger, who thinks I am sleeping, seizes the opportunity to go over HIS system that he plays with his wife, Sandy.

As we are nearing Houston (after four in the morning) I feel I know his system better than my own.

We still have problems. For one thing it is so foggy we can't see very well, and for another both Roger and Sandy are getting a bit tired. Not from driving, you understand; Roger from explaining all the science-fiction meanings of the new bids, and Sandy from trying to remember the new while trying to forget the old.

Roger has enough left for one more brilliancy. Do I have my hotel reservation? Yes, why? Well, it will have the address and we will know which exit to take off the Freeway. Roger is so smart, no wonder Sandy loves him. In fact, they call each other darling all the time except when aggravation sets in. The fact that they were still darling to each other after this experience attests to the strength of their union, their system notwithstanding.

So we get off at Main (the hotel is at Main and Holcomb), but of course, we don't know which way to turn. We turn right. The hotel is to the left. In fact, it is quite a few miles to the left. So after a while we are all on the lookout for Holcomb even though we sometimes miss a street.

Finally, we pass a sign near a turnoff. "What did the sign say?" I ask Roger, who is busily driving up Main. "Holcomb," he answers.

THE SEMIFINALS
We drew first blood when Ross failed to make a questionable lead-directing double of a cue bid.

Both sides vul.
Dealer North

```
                        North (Eisenberg)
                        ♠ Q J 9 2
                        ♡ A Q 8
                        ◇ K J 10 9 2
                        ♣ 2

    West (Paulsen)                              East (Ross)
    ♠ K 7 6 5                                   ♠ 4 3
    ♡ J 6                                       ♡ K 9 7 4 3 2
    ◇ A 5 4 3                                   ◇ Q 8 7 6
    ♣ 10 4 3                                    ♣ 5

                        South (Me)
                        ♠ A 10 8
                        ♡ 10 5
                        ◇ None
                        ♣ A K Q J 9 8 7 6
```

North	East	South	West
1◇	Pass	3♣	Pass
3 NT	Pass	4♣	Pass
4♡	Pass?	6♣	All Pass

Paulsen led a small spade and that was that. In the other room, hearts were never mentioned and five clubs became the final contract.

Obviously, with a heart lead the slam cannot be made.

In spite of this early setback, Ross did get off a good one-liner.

The whole match was on Vu-Graph. As usual, there were mechanical difficulties relaying the information to the Vu Graph Room, where Peter Pender, Edgar Kaplan, and later Peter Rank, were entertaining the audience with both expert and humorous commentary.

The monitor in our room repeatedly kept asking into her head set, "Jack, are you ready?" Invariably, Jack, the Vu-Graph operator, would not be ready and we would have to wait before playing a card or playing the next hand. Finally , Ross said, "eight ever, Jack never."

After a tough struggle the Grand National team prevailed by a final IMP score of 296-235.

Now for the final match against the winners of the Spingold and Vanderbilt — the Rosenkranz team. The stakes were high, a chance to represent the United States in Manila.

THE FINALS
Right off the bat we knew we were in for a long tough match. Katz-Cohen got to seven clubs on these cards, vulnerable.

North (Cohen)
♠ 10 9 6
♡ A 6 5
◊ A 8 7
♣ K 6 5 4

South (Katz)
♠ None
♡ K 8 4
◊ K Q 9 4
♣ A Q 10 8 3 2

Their bidding:

South	North
1 ◊	1 ♡
3 ♣	4 ♣
4 ♠	4 NT
6 ♣	7 ♣

I am not completely familiar with their "Breakthrough Club" system but I do know that Richard showed a hand that had less than 17 high card points with four diamonds and six clubs.

Larry probably figured (hoped) that Richard had the jack of diamonds instead of the nine in which case the grand slam would have been cold. (Larry knew that Richard was void in spades from his response of six clubs.)

In any case, Katz had to bring in the diamonds. After ruffing the spade lead, he drew trumps in two rounds, led a diamond to the ace, a diamond to the king, my ten falling on the left. After long thought he led a heart to the ace and led a diamond to the nine, which is the correct mathematical play and, worse (or better), it worked.

So they laid another seven club contract on me. Shades of Bermuda. In the other room Wolff-Hamman stopped in six clubs.

The second set of 16 boards was perhaps the most exciting of the match. At one point, our team, down 40 IMPs, shaved the deficit to five, only to lose 35 straight IMPs and wind up 40 IMPs down at the quarter.

And again there was a grand slam, and again Katz-Cohen bid it and again it was in clubs! The hands:

West (Katz)	East (Cohen)
♠ 9 8	♠ A K 7 3
♡ A K 5 2	♡ 10 3
◇ A K	◇ Q 3 2
♣ A Q J 7 4	♣ K 6 5 3
1♣ (artificial)	1♠ (natural)
3♣	4♣
4◇	4♠
4 NT	5♡
5NT	7♣
Pass	

In the other room, Soloway opened the West hand with 2 NT and it was almost impossible to get to seven clubs after that start. Their bidding was:

Soloway	Swanson
2 NT	3 ♣
3 ♡	5 NT*
6 ♣	Pass

*(do you have another suit?)

But Swanson-Soloway fought back by bidding a slam in spades on the following hand, Katz-Cohen stopping in five. As you will soon see, six is no bargain.

Both sides vul.
Dealer South

North
♠ A K 10 6
♡ 6
◇ Q 6 4
♣ 9 8 4 3 2

West
♠ Q 9 3
♡ 5 4 3 2
◇ K 9 2
♣ Q J 10

East
♠ 5 4
♡ Q J 10 9 8 7
◇ 8 7 3
♣ 6 5

South
♠ J 8 7 2
♡ A K
◇ A J 10 5
♣ A K 7

South	North
(Swanson)	(Soloway)
2 NT	3 ♣
3 ♠	4 ♡ (Slam try in spades)
5 ♠	6 ♠
Pass	

Swanson was asking about good trumps, and since Soloway thought he had good ones he bid the slam.

Swanson won the club lead, crossed to the ace of spades, back to the ace of hearts and then led a spade to the ten. After that hurdle, he cashed the king of spades, entered his hand with a club, cashed the ace of hearts, discarding a diamond, and exited with a club, end playing West.

Katz-Cohen actually used a splinter auction to stay out of this one. Their bidding was:

South (Cohen)	North (Katz)
1♣ (17-21)	1♠
3♠	5♡ (singleton)
5♠	Pass

Discovering the duplication in hearts, Cohen gave up on the slam. In this 16 board segment Mohan-Rosenkranz bid to a lovely heart slam that Hamman-Wolff missed. These were the bidder's hands:

Opener (Mohan)	Responder (Rosenkranz)
♠ 5	♠ A J 10 8 4
♡ A K 2	♡ Q 8 7 5 3
◇ J 8 2	◇ A
♣ K Q 8 7 6 2	♣ A 4
1♣	1♠
2♣	2♡
3♣	3◇
3♡	4 NT (Key Card)
5◇ (1 or 4?)	5♡
6♡	

Apparently, Mohan corrected the confusion with his 6♡ bid. Hamman-Wolff had an auction that, out of deference to my teammates, I will not print. (Why am I so good to them? They have all my money!)

The score at half time was Rosenkranz 154 Grand Nationals 101. In the third quarter the good news was that Katz-Cohen finally missed a laydown slam on these cards:

Opener	Responder
♠ Q J 10 9 7 5 2	♠ K
♡ A J	♡ K 9 6 2
◇ K 8	◇ A 7 2
♣ K 5	♣ A 10 7 4 2

Katz	Cohen
1♠	1 NT (Forcing)
3♠	4 NT
5◇	5♠
Pass	

The bad news was that Billy and I missed the same slam. Our bidding was:

Billy	Me
1♠	2♣
2♠	3 NT
4♠	Pass

Then, both Katz and I misdefended a slam:

North-South vul.
Dealer South

                          North
                          ♠ A K 9 8
                          ♡ 7
                          ◊ K 9 5 2
                          ♣ A Q 4 3

West   East
♠ 2   ♠ 10 6 4
♡ Q 5   ♡ A 10 8 6
◊ J 10 6 4   ◊ Q 8 3
♣ K J 10 9 7 2   ♣ 8 6 5

                          South
                          ♠ Q J 7 5 3
                          ♡ K J 9 4 3 2
                          ◊ A 7
                          ♣ None

South	West	North	East
1♠	3♣*	4 NT	Pass
6♣**	Pass	6♠	All Pass

*Always trying
**Ace and a club void

Billy led a trump, and when John Mohan tabled the dummy I
knew my problem was whether or not to duck the inevitable heart
lead off the table. Furthermore, I knew if I ducked, I would have
to do it quickly.

But I needed time to think. I went and got myself a coke. I
monkeyed around with the ice cubes trying to figure out distri-
butions. (I must say I did not consider the actual one.)

I finally decided to return to the table and go up with the ace of
hearts (right play if declarer is 5-4-4-0). (This carefully thought

out play allowed Rosenkranz to table his hand and claim shortly thereafter.)

At the other table, six spades was also reached with hearts again never mentioned. Cohen led a diamond to the king and Katz ducked the heart lead off dummy. Hamman finally put in the jack losing to the queen, and a trump came back, Hamman playing low from dummy. At this point the hand can be defeated if Katz does not play his ten. Follow the play.

If the ten is played as it was, Hamman wins, ruffs a heart, back to the ace of diamonds, ruffs a second heart, ruffs a club, ruffs a third heart, establishing the suit, and ruffs himself back in order to draw the last two trumps.

If the ten is not played, Hamman must win in his hand with an honor to begin ruffing hearts; and after ruffing three hearts, two of them with the ace-king, the ten of trumps becomes the setting trick.

My miseries didn't end there. The next tragedy requires an explanation. Billy has been trying to get me to play some form of D.I. (declarative interrogative) four notrump for years.

I have resisted, fearing I wouldn't recognize his bid, would answer aces, pass, or some such horror. Finally we came to a compromise solution.

We would use 4 NT as D.I. but only if clubs or diamonds was the agreed suit, and only if the weaker of the two hands was using the bid.

The D.I. four notrump is a continuing cue bid without a clearcut control, but with extra values that the weaker hand fancies might be enough for slam. Anyway, that was my understanding.

Finally my big moment came in the match. I picked up:

♠ K Q 8 7 3   ♡ 5 3   ◇ K 8   ♣ K J 10 9.

Billy opened 1♣, I responded 1♠, Billy rebid 3♣ and I raised to 4♣, forcing. He now bid 4◇. Well, if there ever looked like a 4 NT to mean "I have a good hand but certainly no second round heart control," this was it.

I alerted. I was hoping I would be asked what the bid meant. For years I have been asking Garozzo and Belladonna about their non-jump four notrump bids. For years they have both been making semi-circular movements with their right hand. Now I know, finally, what they meant. They meant more bidding was coming, everything would be all right, and don't double because they were going to stop in exactly the right contract.

I was ready with the hand movement. Nobody asked, the rats. Billy rebid 5♣. I passed, content that I had finally used the system as Billy had suggested.

I put my dummy down. Something had gone wrong . . . again. This time Billy had:

♠10 9 2 ♡A Q 2 ◇A ♣A Q 8 5 4 2.

We had missed another slam that Mohan and Bates had breezed into.

Why didn't Billy bid six clubs? He was sure I had forgotten the convention and he thought I was bidding Key Card Blackwood. He was showing me three key cards.

So naturally it was my fault. I had picked the wrong time to remember.

So the third quarter ended with our team down 36 IMPs plus an extra four IMP penalty that Billy and I picked up for slow play. The actual IMP total was 221-181.

You see, John Swanson, you had nothing to worry about. I'm not going to tell everyone about the hand you played in four hearts, making seven, because you didn't hear Paul's opening bid! (Seven hearts was bid and made at the other table after a delicate cue bidding sequence by Mohan-Bates.)

And I also considerately did not mention the time Hamman (who still has my money) did the same thing in the first match. However, that one only cost a game, not a slam.

The last day had come and captain Stern had decided to sit Billy and me out the first 16 boards. Play was to begin at 11:30 A.M. and I had mixed emotions.

First, I was glad I was out so I could watch my beloved Lakers play Detroit on National T.V. Second, I knew we would probably play the last sixteen boards which would mean I would miss the Super Bowl. The sacrifices one must make to try to win a World Championship!

Word reached our team that instead of beginning play at the appointed time, play would begin at 1 p.m. A meeting had been called.

We waited and waited and waited. The Super Bowl started— Halftime, still no word. The game was over, still no word. Finally about five in the afternoon the meeting broke and we were told there would be no more play.

Katz and Cohen, for personal reasons, had dropped off the Rosenkranz team and our team was awarded the victory.

No explanations were given and we all left on the first plane out.

The Grand National Team will be one of the two U.S. teams representing the U.S. in Manila next October.

The defending champions, Paulsen, Ross, Hamilton, Rubin, who added Soloway and Eisenberg, will have to find two other players, because Paul and Billy have opted to play on the Grand National team.

What an ending.

Another Record Down the Tubes

I remember reading somewhere that a declarer once made a small slam in spades with this combined trump holding:

Dummy
♠ K 4 3

West
♠ A 9 8

East
♠ Q J

Declarer
♠ 10 7 6 5 2

It seems that after the opening lead, declarer laid down a side suit ace, as if it were a singleton, and then led a low spade towards dummy where the king-queen of the side suit resided.

West, fearing discards were coming, ran up with the ace of spades thus limiting his side to one trump trick with a combined holding of A Q J 9 8.

I must say I was impressed with the defense. After all it is not easy to take only one trick with that combined trump holding.

However, time passed, and while playing with my former partner, Paul Soloway, the following deal arose:

Neither side vul.
Dealer North

                              North
                              ♠ A K Q 6
                              ♡ K
                              ◇ A Q 10 4
                              ♣ K 7 6 4

West (Paul)   East (me)
♠ J 5 4   ♠ 10 9 8 2
♡ 6 5   ♡ A 10 9 3 2
◇ K J 9 3 2   ◇ 8
♣ Q J 5   ♣ A 9 8

                              South
                              ♠ 7 3
                              ♡ Q J 8 7 4
                              ◇ 7 6 5
                              ♣ 10 3 2

North opened two diamonds showing a strong three-suited hand. South responded two hearts announcing he would like to play in hearts if that happened to be one of North's suits.

No luck. North rebid two spades showing a singleton heart. Not wishing to strap his partner into playing a 4-2 fit, South "rescued" to three clubs. North, reading the situation perfectly, raised to four clubs. South, showing great imagination, passed, and the obvious contract was reached.

Paul made the "normal" lead of the five of clubs! Dummy played low, and perceiving the position with my usual astuteness, I played the eight which lost to the ten.

At trick two a heart was led to the king and ace. Can you see it coming? Of course you can. I played the ace and a club. No book can describe the look that passed between Paul and me as his club honors came tumbling down.

Of course, four clubs was such a gruesome contract that we beat it one trick in spite of ourselves. Paul, once he regained his composure, even managed to pay me a compliment of sorts.

"Edwin", he said, "it was not easy to figure out the only way

that our side could take one trump trick with a combined holding of A Q J 9 8 5, but you managed beautifully."

Fool, didn't he realize that history was in the making. I (we)
may have set a record for futility that will last for years.

Addendum: Not long after the above article was published, a letter
came my way indicating that although I should be proud of my
accomplishments, I really was a piker compared to Don Caton and
his partner, Mike Passell, who were defending one notrump with
this combined spade holding:

North
♠ 7 3

West (Passell)   **East (Caton)**
♠ A K Q 4   ♠ J 10 8 6 5

South
♠ 9 2

It seems that South had opened the bidding one of a suit and
had rebid one notrump over partner's response. East-West, with
their magnificent spade fit, had remained silent.

West led the king of spades and East fearing that South had
Q x played the jack to deny the queen and prevent partner from
underleading in case his original holding was A K x x.

When West saw the jack, he thought that East had started with
J 10 x, and rather than block the suit, he continued with a LOW
spade.

When East saw the low spade, he thought that partner's original
spade holding was K Q 9 4 and rather than block the suit, (East
had an outside entry) played low assuming declarer would win
with the now blank ace.

The end result was that South scored a trick with the doubleton nine of spades and the opponents with a combined holding of
A K Q J 10 8 6 5 4 were unable to prevent the declarer from
taking a trick in this suit at a notrump contract.

As much as I hate to admit it, I think this guy and his partner
have got Paul and me beat.

MELVIN POWERS SELF-IMPROVEMENT LIBRARY

ASTROLOGY

_____ASTROLOGY: HOW TO CHART YOUR HOROSCOPE *Max Heindel* 3.00
_____ASTROLOGY: YOUR PERSONAL SUN-SIGN GUIDE *Beatrice Ryder* 3.00
_____ASTROLOGY FOR EVERYDAY LIVING *Janet Harris* 2.00
_____ASTROLOGY MADE EASY *Astarte* 3.00
_____ASTROLOGY MADE PRACTICAL *Alexandra Kayhle* 3.00
_____ASTROLOGY, ROMANCE, YOU AND THE STARS *Anthony Norvell* 4.00
_____MY WORLD OF ASTROLOGY *Sydney Omarr* 5.00
_____THOUGHT DIAL *Sydney Omarr* 4.00
_____WHAT THE STARS REVEAL ABOUT THE MEN IN YOUR LIFE *Thelma White* 3.00

BRIDGE

_____BRIDGE BIDDING MADE EASY *Edwin B. Kantar* 7.00
_____BRIDGE CONVENTIONS *Edwin B. Kantar* 5.00
_____BRIDGE HUMOR *Edwin B. Kantar* 5.00
_____COMPETITIVE BIDDING IN MODERN BRIDGE *Edgar Kaplan* 4.00
_____DEFENSIVE BRIDGE PLAY COMPLETE *Edwin B. Kantar* 10.00
_____GAMESMAN BRIDGE—Play Better with Kantar *Edwin B. Kantar* 5.00
_____HOW TO IMPROVE YOUR BRIDGE *Alfred Sheinwold* 3.00
_____IMPROVING YOUR BIDDING SKILLS *Edwin B. Kantar* 4.00
_____INTRODUCTION TO DEFENDER'S PLAY *Edwin B. Kantar* 3.00
_____SHORT CUT TO WINNING BRIDGE *Alfred Sheinwold* 3.00
_____TEST YOUR BRIDGE PLAY *Edwin B. Kantar* 3.00
_____VOLUME 2—TEST YOUR BRIDGE PLAY *Edwin B. Kantar* 5.00
_____WINNING DECLARER PLAY *Dorothy Hayden Truscott* 4.00

BUSINESS, STUDY & REFERENCE

_____CONVERSATION MADE EASY *Elliot Russell* 3.00
_____EXAM SECRET *Dennis B. Jackson* 3.00
_____FIX-IT BOOK *Arthur Symons* 2.00
_____HOW TO DEVELOP A BETTER SPEAKING VOICE *M. Hellier* 3.00
_____HOW TO MAKE A FORTUNE IN REAL ESTATE *Albert Winnikoff* 4.00
_____INCREASE YOUR LEARNING POWER *Geoffrey A. Dudley* 3.00
_____MAGIC OF NUMBERS *Robert Tocquet* 2.00
_____PRACTICAL GUIDE TO BETTER CONCENTRATION *Melvin Powers* 3.00
_____PRACTICAL GUIDE TO PUBLIC SPEAKING *Maurice Forley* 3.00
_____7 DAYS TO FASTER READING *William S. Schaill* 3.00
_____SONGWRITERS RHYMING DICTIONARY *Jane Shaw Whitfield* 5.00
_____SPELLING MADE EASY *Lester D. Basch & Dr. Milton Finkelstein* 2.00
_____STUDENT'S GUIDE TO BETTER GRADES *J. A. Rickard* 3.00
_____TEST YOURSELF—Find Your Hidden Talent *Jack Shafer* 3.00
_____YOUR WILL & WHAT TO DO ABOUT IT *Attorney Samuel G. Kling* 3.00

CALLIGRAPHY

_____ADVANCED CALLIGRAPHY *Katherine Jeffares* 7.00
_____CALLIGRAPHER'S REFERENCE BOOK *Anne Leptich & Jacque Evans* 6.00
_____CALLIGRAPHY—The Art of Beautiful Writing *Katherine Jeffares* 7.00
_____CALLIGRAPHY FOR FUN & PROFIT *Anne Leptich & Jacque Evans* 7.00
_____CALLIGRAPHY MADE EASY *Tina Serafini* 7.00

CHESS & CHECKERS

_____BEGINNER'S GUIDE TO WINNING CHESS *Fred Reinfeld* 3.00
_____CHECKERS MADE EASY *Tom Wiswell* 2.00
_____CHESS IN TEN EASY LESSONS *Larry Evans* 3.00
_____CHESS MADE EASY *Milton L. Hanauer* 3.00
_____CHESS PROBLEMS FOR BEGINNERS *edited by Fred Reinfeld* 2.00
_____CHESS SECRETS REVEALED *Fred Reinfeld* 2.00
_____CHESS STRATEGY—An Expert's Guide *Fred Reinfeld* 2.00
_____CHESS TACTICS FOR BEGINNERS *edited by Fred Reinfeld* 3.00
_____CHESS THEORY & PRACTICE *Morry & Mitchell* 2.00
_____HOW TO WIN AT CHECKERS *Fred Reinfeld* 3.00
_____1001 BRILLIANT WAYS TO CHECKMATE *Fred Reinfeld* 4.00
_____1001 WINNING CHESS SACRIFICES & COMBINATIONS *Fred Reinfeld* 4.00
_____SOVIET CHESS *Edited by R. G. Wade* 3.00

COOKERY & HERBS

____CULPEPER'S HERBAL REMEDIES *Dr. Nicholas Culpeper* 3.00
____FAST GOURMET COOKBOOK *Poppy Cannon* 2.50
____GINSENG The Myth & The Truth *Joseph P. Hou* 3.00
____HEALING POWER OF HERBS *May Bethel* 3.00
____HEALING POWER OF NATURAL FOODS *May Bethel* 3.00
____HERB HANDBOOK *Dawn MacLeod* 3.00
____HERBS FOR COOKING AND HEALING *Dr. Donald Law* 2.00
____HERBS FOR HEALTH—How to Grow & Use Them *Louise Evans Doole* 3.00
____HOME GARDEN COOKBOOK—Delicious Natural Food Recipes *Ken Kraft* 3.00
____MEDICAL HERBALIST *edited by Dr. J. R. Yemm* 3.00
____NATURAL FOOD COOKBOOK *Dr. Harry C. Bond* 3.00
____NATURE'S MEDICINES *Richard Lucas* 3.00
____VEGETABLE GARDENING FOR BEGINNERS *Hugh Wiberg* 2.00
____VEGETABLES FOR TODAY'S GARDENS *R. Milton Carleton* 2.00
____VEGETARIAN COOKERY *Janet Walker* 4.00
____VEGETARIAN COOKING MADE EASY & DELECTABLE *Veronica Vezza* 3.00
____VEGETARIAN DELIGHTS—A Happy Cookbook for Health *K. R. Mehta* 2.00
____VEGETARIAN GOURMET COOKBOOK *Joyce McKinnel* 3.00

GAMBLING & POKER

____ADVANCED POKER STRATEGY & WINNING PLAY *A. D. Livingston* 3.00
____HOW NOT TO LOSE AT POKER *Jeffrey Lloyd Castle* 3.00
____HOW TO WIN AT DICE GAMES *Skip Frey* 3.00
____HOW TO WIN AT POKER *Terence Reese & Anthony T. Watkins* 3.00
____SECRETS OF WINNING POKER *George S. Coffin* 3.00
____WINNING AT CRAPS *Dr. Lloyd T. Commins* 3.00
____WINNING AT GIN *Chester Wander & Cy Rice* 3.00
____WINNING AT POKER—An Expert's Guide *John Archer* 3.00
____WINNING AT 21—An Expert's Guide *John Archer* 4.00
____WINNING POKER SYSTEMS *Norman Zadeh* 3.00

HEALTH

____BEE POLLEN *Lynda Lyngheim & Jack Scagnetti* 3.00
____DR. LINDNER'S SPECIAL WEIGHT CONTROL METHOD *P. G. Lindner, M.D.* 1.50
____HELP YOURSELF TO BETTER SIGHT *Margaret Darst Corbett* 3.00
____HOW TO IMPROVE YOUR VISION *Dr. Robert A. Kraskin* 3.00
____HOW YOU CAN STOP SMOKING PERMANENTLY *Ernest Caldwell* 3.00
____MIND OVER PLATTER *Peter G. Lindner, M.D.* 3.00
____NATURE'S WAY TO NUTRITION & VIBRANT HEALTH *Robert J. Scrutton* 3.00
____NEW CARBOHYDRATE DIET COUNTER *Patti Lopez-Pereira* 1.50
____QUICK & EASY EXERCISES FOR FACIAL BEAUTY *Judy Smith-deal* 2.00
____QUICK & EASY EXERCISES FOR FIGURE BEAUTY *Judy Smith-deal* 2.00
____REFLEXOLOGY *Dr. Maybelle Segal* 3.00
____REFLEXOLOGY FOR GOOD HEALTH *Anna Kaye & Don C. Matchan* 3.00
____YOU CAN LEARN TO RELAX *Dr. Samuel Gutwirth* 3.00
____YOUR ALLERGY—What To Do About It *Allan Knight, M.D.* 3.00

HOBBIES

____BEACHCOMBING FOR BEGINNERS *Norman Hickin* 2.00
____BLACKSTONE'S MODERN CARD TRICKS *Harry Blackstone* 3.00
____BLACKSTONE'S SECRETS OF MAGIC *Harry Blackstone* 3.00
____COIN COLLECTING FOR BEGINNERS *Burton Hobson & Fred Reinfeld* 3.00
____ENTERTAINING WITH ESP *Tony 'Doc' Shiels* 2.00
____400 FASCINATING MAGIC TRICKS YOU CAN DO *Howard Thurston* 3.00
____HOW I TURN JUNK INTO FUN AND PROFIT *Sari* 3.00
____HOW TO WRITE A HIT SONG & SELL IT *Tommy Boyce* 7.00
____JUGGLING MADE EASY *Rudolf Dittrich* 2.00
____MAGIC FOR ALL AGES *Walter Gibson* 4.00
____MAGIC MADE EASY *Byron Wels* 2.00
____STAMP COLLECTING FOR BEGINNERS *Burton Hobson* 2.00

HORSE PLAYERS' WINNING GUIDES

____BETTING HORSES TO WIN *Les Conklin* 3.00
____ELIMINATE THE LOSERS *Bob McKnight* 3.00

HOW TO RAISE AN EMOTIONALLY HEALTHY, HAPPY CHILD *A. Ellis* 3.00
IMPOTENCE & FRIGIDITY *Edwin W. Hirsch, M.D.* 3.00
SEX WITHOUT GUILT *Albert Ellis, Ph.D.* 3.00
SEXUALLY ADEQUATE MALE *Frank S. Caprio, M.D.* 3.00

MELVIN POWERS' MAIL ORDER LIBRARY
HOW TO GET RICH IN MAIL ORDER *Melvin Powers* 10.00
HOW TO WRITE A GOOD ADVERTISEMENT *Victor O. Schwab* 15.00
WORLD WIDE MAIL ORDER SHOPPER'S GUIDE *Eugene V. Moller* 5.00

METAPHYSICS & OCCULT
BOOK OF TALISMANS, AMULETS & ZODIACAL GEMS *William Pavitt* 4.00
CONCENTRATION—A Guide to Mental Mastery *Mouni Sadhu* 3.00
CRITIQUES OF GOD *Edited by Peter Angeles* 7.00
DREAMS & OMENS REVEALED *Fred Gettings* 3.00
EXTRA-TERRESTRIAL INTELLIGENCE—The First Encounter 6.00
FORTUNE TELLING WITH CARDS *P. Foli* 3.00
HANDWRITING ANALYSIS MADE EASY *John Marley* 3.00
HANDWRITING TELLS *Nadya Olyanova* 5.00
HOW TO UNDERSTAND YOUR DREAMS *Geoffrey A. Dudley* 3.00
ILLUSTRATED YOGA *William Zorn* 3.00
IN DAYS OF GREAT PEACE *Mouni Sadhu* 3.00
KING SOLOMON'S TEMPLE IN THE MASONIC TRADITION *Alex Horne* 5.00
LSD—THE AGE OF MIND *Bernard Roseman* 2.00
MAGICIAN—His training and work *W. E. Butler* 3.00
MEDITATION *Mouni Sadhu* 5.00
MODERN NUMEROLOGY *Morris C. Goodman* 3.00
NUMEROLOGY—ITS FACTS AND SECRETS *Ariel Yvon Taylor* 3.00
NUMEROLOGY MADE EASY *W. Mykian* 3.00
PALMISTRY MADE EASY *Fred Gettings* 3.00
PALMISTRY MADE PRACTICAL *Elizabeth Daniels Squire* 3.00
PALMISTRY SECRETS REVEALED *Henry Frith* 3.00
PROPHECY IN OUR TIME *Martin Ebon* 2.50
PSYCHOLOGY OF HANDWRITING *Nadya Olyanova* 3.00
SUPERSTITION—Are you superstitious? *Eric Maple* 2.00
TAROT *Mouni Sadhu* 6.00
TAROT OF THE BOHEMIANS *Papus* 5.00
WAYS TO SELF-REALIZATION *Mouni Sadhu* 3.00
WHAT YOUR HANDWRITING REVEALS *Albert E. Hughes* 2.00
WITCHCRAFT, MAGIC & OCCULTISM—A Fascinating History *W. B. Crow* 5.00
WITCHCRAFT—THE SIXTH SENSE *Justine Glass* 4.00
WORLD OF PSYCHIC RESEARCH *Hereward Carrington* 2.00

SELF-HELP & INSPIRATIONAL
DAILY POWER FOR JOYFUL LIVING *Dr. Donald Curtis* 3.00
DYNAMIC THINKING *Melvin Powers* 2.00
EXUBERANCE—Your Guide to Happiness & Fulfillment *Dr. Paul Kurtz* 3.00
GREATEST POWER IN THE UNIVERSE *U. S. Andersen* 5.00
GROW RICH WHILE YOU SLEEP *Ben Sweetland* 3.00
GROWTH THROUGH REASON *Albert Ellis, Ph.D.* 4.00
GUIDE TO DEVELOPING YOUR POTENTIAL *Herbert A. Otto, Ph.D.* 3.00
GUIDE TO LIVING IN BALANCE *Frank S. Caprio, M.D.* 2.00
HELPING YOURSELF WITH APPLIED PSYCHOLOGY *R. Henderson* 2.00
HELPING YOURSELF WITH PSYCHIATRY *Frank S. Caprio, M.D.* 2.00
HOW TO ATTRACT GOOD LUCK *A. H. Z. Carr* 4.00
HOW TO CONTROL YOUR DESTINY *Norvell* 3.00
HOW TO DEVELOP A WINNING PERSONALITY *Martin Panzer* 3.00
HOW TO DEVELOP AN EXCEPTIONAL MEMORY *Young & Gibson* 4.00
HOW TO OVERCOME YOUR FEARS *M. P. Leahy, M.D.* 3.00
HOW YOU CAN HAVE CONFIDENCE AND POWER *Les Giblin* 3.00
HUMAN PROBLEMS & HOW TO SOLVE THEM *Dr. Donald Curtis* 4.00
I CAN *Ben Sweetland* 4.00
I WILL *Ben Sweetland* 3.00
LEFT-HANDED PEOPLE *Michael Barsley* 4.00

_____MAGIC IN YOUR MIND *U. S. Andersen* 5.00
_____MAGIC OF THINKING BIG *Dr. David J. Schwartz* 3.00
_____MAGIC POWER OF YOUR MIND *Walter M. Germain* 4.00
_____MENTAL POWER THROUGH SLEEP SUGGESTION *Melvin Powers* 3.00
_____NEW GUIDE TO RATIONAL LIVING *Albert Ellis, Ph.D. & R. Harper, Ph.D.* 3.00
_____OUR TROUBLED SELVES *Dr. Allan Fromme* 3.00
_____PSYCHO-CYBERNETICS *Maxwell Maltz, M.D.* 2.00
_____SCIENCE OF MIND IN DAILY LIVING *Dr. Donald Curtis* 3.00
_____SECRET OF SECRETS *U. S. Andersen* 5.00
_____SECRET POWER OF THE PYRAMIDS *U. S. Andersen* 5.00
_____STUTTERING AND WHAT YOU CAN DO ABOUT IT *W. Johnson, Ph.D.* 2.50
_____SUCCESS-CYBERNETICS *U. S. Andersen* 4.00
_____10 DAYS TO A GREAT NEW LIFE *William E. Edwards* 3.00
_____THINK AND GROW RICH *Napoleon Hill* 3.00
_____THREE MAGIC WORDS *U. S. Andersen* 5.00
_____TREASURY OF COMFORT *edited by Rabbi Sidney Greenberg* 5.00
_____TREASURY OF THE ART OF LIVING *Sidney S. Greenberg* 5.00
_____YOU ARE NOT THE TARGET *Laura Huxley* 4.00
_____YOUR SUBCONSCIOUS POWER *Charles M. Simmons* 4.00
_____YOUR THOUGHTS CAN CHANGE YOUR LIFE *Dr. Donald Curtis* 4.00

SPORTS
_____BICYCLING FOR FUN AND GOOD HEALTH *Kenneth E. Luther* 2.00
_____BILLIARDS—Pocket • Carom • Three Cushion *Clive Cottingham, Jr.* 3.00
_____CAMPING-OUT 101 Ideas & Activities *Bruno Knobel* 2.00
_____COMPLETE GUIDE TO FISHING *Vlad Evanoff* 2.00
_____HOW TO IMPROVE YOUR RACQUETBALL *Lubarsky, Kaufman, & Scagnetti* 3.00
_____HOW TO WIN AT POCKET BILLIARDS *Edward D. Knuchell* 4.00
_____JOY OF WALKING *Jack Scagnetti* 3.00
_____LEARNING & TEACHING SOCCER SKILLS *Eric Worthington* 3.00
_____MOTORCYCLING FOR BEGINNERS *I. G. Edmonds* 3.00
_____RACQUETBALL FOR WOMEN *Toni Hudson, Jack Scagnetti & Vince Rondone* 3.00
_____RACQUETBALL MADE EASY *Steve Lubarsky, Rod Delson & Jack Scagnetti* 3.00
_____SECRET OF BOWLING STRIKES *Dawson Taylor* 3.00
_____SECRET OF PERFECT PUTTING *Horton Smith & Dawson Taylor* 3.00
_____SOCCER—The game & how to play it *Gary Rosenthal* 3.00
_____STARTING SOCCER *Edward F. Dolan, Jr.* 3.00
_____TABLE TENNIS MADE EASY *Johnny Leach* 2.00

TENNIS LOVERS' LIBRARY
_____BEGINNER'S GUIDE TO WINNING TENNIS *Helen Hull Jacobs* 2.00
_____HOW TO BEAT BETTER TENNIS PLAYERS *Loring Fiske* 4.00
_____HOW TO IMPROVE YOUR TENNIS—Style, Strategy & Analysis *C. Wilson* 2.00
_____INSIDE TENNIS—Techniques of Winning *Jim Leighton* 3.00
_____PLAY TENNIS WITH ROSEWALL *Ken Rosewall* 2.00
_____PSYCH YOURSELF TO BETTER TENNIS *Dr. Walter A. Luszki* 2.00
_____SUCCESSFUL TENNIS *Neale Fraser* 2.00
_____TENNIS FOR BEGINNERS *Dr. H. A. Murray* 2.00
_____TENNIS MADE EASY *Joel Brecheen* 2.00
_____WEEKEND TENNIS—How to have fun & win at the same time *Bill Talbert* 3.00
_____WINNING WITH PERCENTAGE TENNIS—Smart Strategy *Jack Lowe* 2.00

WILSHIRE PET LIBRARY
_____DOG OBEDIENCE TRAINING *Gust Kessopulos* 4.00
_____DOG TRAINING MADE EASY & FUN *John W. Kellogg* 3.00
_____HOW TO BRING UP YOUR PET DOG *Kurt Unkelbach* 2.00
_____HOW TO RAISE & TRAIN YOUR PUPPY *Jeff Griffen* 2.00
_____PIGEONS: HOW TO RAISE & TRAIN THEM *William H. Allen, Jr.* 2.00

*The books listed above can be obtained from your book dealer or directly from
Melvin Powers. When ordering, please remit 50¢ per book postage & handling.
Send for our free illustrated catalog of self-improvement books.*

Melvin Powers
12015 Sherman Road, No. Hollywood, California 91605